"In *Testimonies of*  stories that are e grace. Heartbreak testimonies of abo... tug at your soul and pose the question, 'Is the church doing everything we can to extend grace to the most broken and downtrodden?' Dr. Brown's Biblical wisdom brings forth validation to pain and the reminder of God's unconditional love, to release you from a life of shame and into a life of freedom. Readers will identify with what Jesus calls 'the least of these' and will cheer with the power of God's redeeming love. Anyone who has ever felt 'less than' needs to read this book!"

Renee Nickell, Bestselling Author of *Always My Hero: The Road to Hope & Healing Following My Brother's Death in Afghanistan*

"Such a great book. I loved Chris' first book and really looked forward to reading his new one. I was not disappointed. As a Christian and knowing my own struggle in life, it's always uplifting and helpful to hear/read the struggle that others have overcome in their own lives. I think a lot of times the word Christian gets a bad rap. It does not mean we are perfect, or think that we are. It's the opposite, we know that we are broken and need help to make it through life on a daily basis. If you want to know what God's grace and mercy looks like, read *Testimonies of Grace*."

Brandi Atchison, Owner of Shades of Pemberley Bookstore and Book Reviewer for Land + Lake Magazine

"Both hands in the air! *Testimonies of Grace* honors the bloody mud at the foot of the cross. Bravely told, these raw testimonies debunk the faceless, artificial sheen of modern Christianity as a world religion and rightly return focus to the face and eyes, the wild, radical love of Jesus the Christ... hope and full redemption available to ANYONE who should call upon His Name."

Jeremy Collins, President and Founder of Three Circles Foundation

"*Testimonies of Grace* is full of incredible personal stories that demonstrate God's deep love for us and His pursuit of us even while we are not pursuing Him. Every story is filled with such honesty of how our sins draw us away from God but how we are never drawn out of reach of His forgiveness. Each chapter offers resources to extend that help and hope found in Jesus for whatever struggles you may be facing."

Cathryn Buse, Christian apologist and founder of Defend the Faith Ministry

"*Testimonies of Grace* showcases Chris Brown's ability to capture a person's life story in such a way that Jesus gets the Glory He deserves. Readers will identify, in some part, with one or more of the participants. An added bonus is the list of scripture and book references at the end of each testimony to help the reader dig deeper into finding the help and encouragement they need."

Peggy Weidert, Owner of The Mustard Seed Christian Bookstore

"'People never change' … at least that's what we've been told. People may not change, but the power of the Holy Spirit transforms lives when we allow him to. Through compelling stories, *Testimonies of Grace* gives the reader access to the inside world of broken lives put back together by Jesus. *Testimonies of Grace* is an inspiring account of eight remarkable journeys, each one starting off in unique and different circumstances, but all leading to a restored relationship with God. Finally, reading *Testimonies of Grace* was also a stirring and encouraging reminder that God is still at work in my life as well!"

Hal Ward, Founder of Vino Nuevo Ministry

"*Testimonies of Grace* reminds us to never give up on anyone. With God, there is always hope. It is a reminder of the Good Shepherd who searches for and brings the lost sheep home. As Paul says, 'I am the worst of them.' We need to all remember that we are all the worst of them and not judge others. We have not walked in their shoes. Dr. Chris Brown very aptly weaves these stories of redemption with threads of God's grace, hope and salvation. These stories show the power of prayer and how we all are given opportunities to plant seeds, but only God can change hearts. These stories motivate us to strive to do a better job of listening to God's voice when He prompts us to help those who society says are beyond help because with God all things are possible! No one is beyond hope!"

Mindy van Dyke, Owner of Stepping Stones Christian Bookstores

"With brutal honesty and intense vulnerability, *Testimonies of Grace* is a beacon of hope for the lost, and a reminder that there is no soul too far gone that the Lord cannot redeem. A must-read for a healthy dose of empathy and insight into the mysterious workings of God as the lost reach rock bottom and He meets them where they are. Not only is it a message of how lives were changed, but how God - through different people and situations - was at work in their hearts long before their eyes were opened to their ultimate need for Him."

Becca Weidel, Christian Book Reviewer at The Becca Files

"In *Testimonies of Grace*, you will find eight wonderful testimonies revealing the love of God. The testimonies will inspire you to write your own life-changing story. Testimonies are evidence of the miracle-working power of God which changes lives. Corrie Ten Boom often recalled her sister's words, 'There is no pit so deep that God's love is not deeper still.' You will find yourself thanking God out loud for His loving kindness and mercy. Each testimony reveals a different aspect of God's unfolding and eternal love for us."

Ivan Tait, Founder and CEO of What Matters Ministries and Missions

TESTIMONIES
of GRACE

DR. CHRIS BROWN

ISBN 978-0-578-73890-1 (paperback)

ISBN 978-0-578-73891-8 (digital)

Independently published by Child of Grace Books
www.childofgracebooks.com
info@childofgracebooks.com

Holy Bible, New International Version*, NIV*, Copyright © 1973, 1978, 1984, 2011 by Biblica, Inc.* Used by permission. All rights reserved worldwide.

Acknowledgments

First and foremost, I must give all thanks and all glory to my Lord and Savior Jesus Christ, through whom all things are possible. I must acknowledge all eight contributors to this book, who each poured out their hearts in real vulnerability so that their stories might bring glory to God and healing to those who read this book. I am eternally grateful to my wife and children, who patiently allowed me to spend so much time and energy on this effort. This project would not be what it is today without Sarah Annerton, who always provides me with amazing artwork and advice. And finally I must recognize my editor, Jennifer Kelly, and the readers of several early drafts; they all made this project much better than it would have been without them.

Table of Contents

Preface

We pass by people every day without knowing what they're going through or what their stories are. We see them at work. We share a pew with them at church. We see them at the grocery store or the neighborhood park. Behind each smiling face is a life story. What would you discover if you knew those stories? How would you interact with them if you knew what they have endured? How would your own life be impacted if you saw more than a face?

Testimonies of Grace is here to tell eight of those stories. They are Ashleigh Grace, Whit, Tiffany, Barry, Lauren, Ken, Sadie, and Mark; four men and four women, some young and some not so young, some raised in the church, some not, some single and some married (Barry and Lauren are married to each other). These are eight people who you might not give a second look if you passed them on the street, yet they each have incredible stories of God's amazing grace in their lives. Here, you will find heartbreak and pain, but also the encouragement and hope that comes with faith in Jesus Christ. If you're not so sure about Jesus, just read on and take in these real accounts of encounters with Him.

Through interviews and some of their own writing, each story is told from the point of view of the individual.

11

PREFACE

These are true stories and real events. In some cases, names and details have been changed to protect the innocent (and the guilty). These eight stories illustrate the ways in which God moves and works in individual lives. Together, they show His grace in every situation. This book will encourage the saints, challenge the religious, and give the skeptics something to ponder. All are welcome here.

More to Think About

Following each story is a section called "More to Think About." This section will provide concrete steps and resources that can help if you or someone you know is currently in a situation similar to the one you've just read about. In each section, you will find practical ways to apply what you've just read in a testimony. Each section will include scripture to meditate on and the opening of a prayer you can make your own. At the end of the book is a comprehensive list of the books, resources, and references mentioned in each chapter. The story is just the beginning – what you do with it is what counts.

Innocence Lost – Ashleigh Grace's Story

When I was in elementary school, I started having the same recurring dream. In it, I would walk toward my great-grandmother's home, across a bridge over the creek, and into an old barn. Inside, I would realize it wasn't a barn but a slaughterhouse – a human slaughterhouse. Each time, I would wake up with the image of slaughtered people on hooks in this old barn. I don't know if the dream involved my mean great-grandmother because we thought she might actually be a witch, but I do know that I always associated that dream with the realization that I was being molested. It was not so much the realization that it was happening, but the understanding that I was being violated and it was wrong. It went on for years, from the time I was very young until middle school. My violators were people I knew: an uncle, my cousins, my step-mom's son, and a friend of my dad. When I was in fifth grade, my cousin raped me. It was not just the molestation I had known for so long; this time it was a violent rape. I don't know why I didn't fight back, probably out of pure shock, but I just laid there. In the end, there was so much blood it looked like someone had been murdered in that room. I know my aunt knew what had happened because she was the one who cleaned it up -- and covered it up. I told my mom and she told me to be sure I didn't tell my grandmother because it would upset her. I had been violently abused by my cousin and my mom's biggest concern was not upsetting my grandmother. From there, my life tumbled deeper and deeper into chaos, until many years later when I came to know Jesus Christ.

I was born in the South in 1978. My mother has been married thirteen times, including my father. He cheated on her and they divorced when I was three years old. She never forgave him for it. Until the day he died, he never said anything bad about her. We weren't dirt poor, but my mom always struggled; my dad always seemed to have money, but that was all he gave me growing up. He was a Vietnam veteran but he never talked about his experience in the war. After they divorced, my mom didn't want to keep anything from that marriage, including me. I ended up staying some with my dad's mother and then spent some time with his sister. That's when the molestation started. I'm sure my aunt knew my uncle was molesting me, but she kept it quiet. I don't know who all knew, really, but the family members and friends molesting me couldn't have been a complete mystery. I guess a child nobody really wanted was easy to abuse without anyone caring too much. I had a truly evil stepmom too; she actually kidnapped me for a couple of days after my dad decided to divorce her. She brought me back without really doing anything harmful to me. The molestation, though, went on for years, from preschool until fifth grade. I had moved back in with my mom for a little while when the rape happened. I was angry at the world. I didn't understand why that had happened to me. I began to put up so many emotional walls because I didn't want to feel anything anymore. After being abused so much, I felt like maybe abuse was just what I was made for. I'm not sure exactly when I started cutting myself, I just knew that I would rather feel physical pain than emotional pain. Cutting gave me that release; otherwise, I just made myself be numb to everything.

After the rape, I was sexually active. It was what I knew. My family members were doing what they knew as well. My great-grandmother really was cruel and I believe she was involved in occult practices. My mom was literally the milkman's baby. The uncle who molested me is dead now; I don't know whether he attacked anyone else. Now that I understand more about generational curses[1], I realize how many of them are in my family. I know a lot of the things I've been diagnosed with like ADHD and Bipolar Disorder came from generational curses too. I still don't like going back where I grew up to visit, but I feel like I need to go and pray for these curses to be broken.

INNOCENCE LOST – ASHLEIGH GRACE'S STORY

I was a little hooligan in middle school, sexually active and already involved in substance abuse. My dad was a lot more concerned about something else though. He was a member of the Ku Klux Klan. The KKK was active in the area, regularly burning crosses and holding open meetings. My dad could overlook everything except the fact that I liked little black boys. When I was in sixth or seventh grade, I invited some black boys to my birthday party and he had me committed to a mental health facility because of it. In the middle of arguing about it, I picked up a gun that I thought was loaded, pointed it at my dad, and pulled the trigger. Thankfully, it really wasn't loaded, but, needless to say, that episode put a strain on our relationship from then on. It is not unusual for victims of trauma to become violent themselves; that was the case for me for many years. Impulsive and often violent outbursts were a regular part of my life.

I spent my first week at the mental facility in a straightjacket but, after that, I settled in and came to like the place. They seemed like they really wanted me to tell them something crazy, so I said I had shot a man and dumped him in a quarry. I totally made it up, but my parents and the facility still had to go check it out. Living at the facility was honestly the happiest part of my childhood because it was the only time that I was sure I was safe. It didn't take too long before I got kicked out, though. A friend on the staff said I could hit her if I wanted to; I did it and they kicked me out. I had felt a real bond with her and I really didn't want to leave the facility, but I just acted on impulse like I did so often. After I got kicked out, I went back to my grandmother's house and my destructive lifestyle. Later, I found out that most of the facility staff were alcoholics and the director even had some DUIs on her record.

My lifestyle of sex and drugs continued in high school. I was so addicted to drugs that it was the first thing I thought about every morning when I woke up. My academic career got cut short my sophomore year when I got kicked out of school for assaulting a police officer on school property. He was trying to arrest me for selling marijuana and I knocked him out cold. That officer is now the chief of police in a small town in that area. I was fifteen years old when I got expelled, and, by age sixteen, I was living on my own. I did eventually get my GED.

My first son was born in 1998. I didn't really love his dad and our son was not planned. I was young, I didn't know anything about kids and I completely freaked out. I never married his dad, and, when our son was six months old, I caught his dad cheating with a friend and left him. When our son was three years old, his dad died from diabetes. He had already gone blind from it. One day, he fell in the shower; by the time his mom and our son found him, he was brain-damaged and didn't live long after that. I love my son, but it has always been a difficult relationship. I was so young when I had him that we basically grew up together.

My son did help another difficult relationship though. My biracial son melted my Klansman father's heart. My dad fell in love with my baby as soon as he saw him. Ultimately, my father met an untimely end as well, his death occurring under suspicious circumstances while married to his third wife. Near the end of his life, in our last conversation, I talked to him about the Lord and he said he was a believer. He also said three words I needed to hear: I forgive you. He forgave me for pointing a gun at him and pulling the trigger as a teenager, and, until he said it, I hadn't realized how desperately I needed that forgiveness.

After I left my son's father, we moved in with an aunt and her girlfriend. That aunt was a fun adult, but not a good adult. She was the first person I did cocaine with. I was mad at men and living with two lesbians, so I decided to give that lifestyle a try myself. I went to gay bars, loved to watch the drag queen shows, and even had a girlfriend at one point, but I realized pretty quickly that I wasn't really gay and that lifestyle was not for me. My aunt and her girlfriend got me a job working with them manufacturing

DVDs. I was making about $500 per week. Pretty soon, I found a profession that was a lot more lucrative: working as a stripper. My first night, I made $1,000. That was in 1999. Stripping would be my job for the next ten years, throughout my first marriage and the birth of a second son in 2005.

I was still impulsive and violent, and still a drug addict, and making a lot of money stripping only made that worse. I would do thousands of dollars of drugs in a day with friends from the strip club. I quickly shrunk down to an 85-pound crackhead. I'm surprised my heart still works at all after all the drugs I did. At the club, I was as wild as ever. When the presidential dollar coins became popular, a guy gave me one, but I thought it was a quarter; I took off my shoe and beat the crap out of him with it. My friends jumped in too, like always. A couple of us got in a serious car accident while we were driving high. We were riding in a little red pickup; I had fallen asleep, but I woke up with my face in the floorboard while the truck flipped in the air. It landed upside down in a ditch; we walked away from it with no real injuries. I was a violent drug addict and totally out of control, but still God watched over me.

I married my first husband in 2001. He was a big gangster from the Midwest who robbed armored cars. He was 23 years older than me. I kept stripping and he kept making money as a gangster and we lived a lifestyle of violence and addiction throughout our four-year marriage. I cheated on him all the time. At the end of our marriage, I had met a boy at the club I worked in and decided to go to Atlanta with him. He was a dope boy and we got pulled over on the way back with several kilos in the car. We sat in jail for a week before he paid them off and got us out. I could have done twenty years for that. Later, I found out that the cops who had arrested us got busted with a few kilos themselves. That triggered a re-investigation of everyone they had arrested; I was the only one not called back to court. The dope boy I went there with got nine years on paper after the new investigation. My name had miraculously disappeared from the record.

After I got back home from the ill-fated trip to Atlanta, I had one final violent encounter with my first husband when he tried to kill me. He held a gun to my head and pulled the trigger. Thank God he was a terrible shot; I felt the heat of the bullet as it went past my eyes, but he missed me. That was the end of that marriage. He didn't know I was pregnant and he only learned much later that he has a son.

When I was little, I had one aunt who would take me to church sometimes. I walked down the aisle in her evangelical church and asked Jesus to come into my heart. I expected some kind of big bang, but nothing like that happened. I didn't feel a whole lot different at the time. It would be many years before I really got to know Jesus Christ, but, despite everything that happened after the day I walked down the aisle as a child and despite everything I did after that, I believe I was saved that day and He had His hand on my life. Otherwise, there is no way I would still be alive.

I moved to another state with my younger son and got a pharmacy certificate at a local community college. I never used it though; stripping made a lot more money than working at a drug store. Before I had a chance to even try to use my certificate, I was involved in a car wreck that should have killed me. I was driving down the interstate on my way back home when it started raining. I lost control of the vehicle and should have ended up in the river; I did have severe head trauma as my head struck multiple trees, but, miraculously, I survived. Some people from up north had been behind me and they stayed with me until the paramedics came; I only stayed in the local hospital one night because I didn't have insurance. After I got back to my new home, I ended up in a hospital for a week. I recovered physically, but, since the wreck, my memory is not very good. I can remember events but I have a really hard time remembering dates and time periods. The years I can remember are when I was born, my kids were born, or I got married. Everything else I know happened but it's difficult to say exactly when. The wreck also made it hard to use the pharmacy certificate I had earned because of the memory problems it caused.

I met my second husband, an immigrant from Latin America, after my wreck. He already had kids and I did not want any more kids, so we never had any children together. I met him through a friend, and, on our first date, he said I couldn't be his lady and work as a stripper. I never went back to the club after that. I have learned a lot about the word perseverance[2] as I continue to pray for him to come to know the Lord as I do now. Neither of us was living for the Lord when we got married, and, despite everything that happened in that ten years, I still pray that he will come to know Jesus.

My return to the Lord happened through my younger son. We were zoned for a public school that had a lot of problems. He had been bullied a little bit before, but, when he was in first grade, I witnessed another boy punch the school's librarian. She said she couldn't do anything about it. I couldn't believe it. They tolerated violence from the kids toward the staff and didn't do anything. I had an accountant friend whose son went to a local Christian school, so I checked it out and we decided to put my son there.

It wasn't long before I decided to go to the church that my son's school was a part of. The Holy Spirit was drawing me back to Him.[3] I had tried going to a couple of other churches, but I never really connected. I knew so little about Christianity that I didn't even know there were Christian schools before my son went to one. I had always believed God was real and I had walked down the aisle when I was little, but I didn't know I could have a relationship with God[4]. For the first time, I went to church and really felt His love in every encounter. I got to know the pastors and saw the love of Jesus in every one of them. I was practically adopted by a lady in the church who became a true friend and mentor to me. I learned about the Holy Spirit and what He could do in my life.

I was driving my son to swim one day when I just started crying. I couldn't stop crying and I didn't know why. The Holy Spirit told me to go and pray with one of the pastors. I didn't want to go; I said I would drive by, and, if her car was there, I would go in. Of course, she was there and I went in to see her. I told her I didn't know why I was there, but I just couldn't stop crying. She prayed over me in the power of the Holy Spirit and my life has not been the same since. The Bible tells us about many different prayers for deliverance[5]: deliverance from infirmities, deliverance from sin, deliverance from enemies and evil, and deliverance for spiritual freedom. I needed them all. She prayed for deliverance from everything that had oppressed me all of those years and I walked out completely changed by His power.

Everyone has been able to see the change in my life since that day. I had still been cutting myself until then, but that curse was broken that day. My impulsive and violent tendencies subsided after that day. I didn't struggle with substance abuse after that day. My mental health is better and I am off most of the medications I had been on for bipolar disorder. I quit watching secular TV and listening to secular music. Music has always moved me. It used to just be Tupac, but I discovered there is good Christian rap like Lecrae[6]; his song "Take Me as I Am" touched my soul and is still my favorite. Jesus met me where I was, He took me as I was, and now I don't know how people live without Him.

I feel like I'm just now learning how to love and be loved. I went on a mission trip to Guatemala, where my church supports three orphanages and a school. Many of the children in these orphanages were terribly abused. Some were left in the garbage dump as babies, some were used as prostitutes from a young age, and one was being grown just to harvest organs from. Their stories are all heartbreaking, yet they have all learned a new life of being loved and cared for. As we ministered to these children, I heard my pastors speak about love and I realized there was so much I didn't know. More than anything, I know that God is faithful.

Later, I went on a mission trip to Idaho to serve a refugee community and it was absolutely life-changing. I saw one of my pastors with her family and she came across as nothing but love. I wondered if it was real; I had never seen a family act like that with each other. They truly loved each other and helped me learn to love. As our group went to show love to the community of mostly Muslim African refugees, I saw that it was possible to love and serve people we had nothing in common with; we loved them with no strings attached because they had nothing material to offer us. It was the love of Jesus in action.

I am still growing in Christ and that is what is so beautiful. I am blessed and highly favored and I see life so differently now as the Lord continues to slowly develop things in me. I hated people before, even saying as much at my church, but, when you see people who are so genuine and just love the Lord, it changes your perspective. I have started helping with the volunteers who work on the church grounds: I'm a country girl who likes to get her hands dirty after all. I have gone on "treasure hunts[7]" where we pray for the Holy Spirit to lead us to specific people, an amazing experience every single time. Now, I love to laugh with my church friends and a widower old enough to be my father makes me laugh more than anyone. I have taken the mother of one of my second husband's children with me to church. Even in the times when I have tremendous struggles, the Lord is with me. Even when I have wanted to do the wrong thing, God has put up obstacles and roadblocks to keep me from really messing up.

I always said that I didn't want to get divorced again. I don't want to end up with thirteen marriages like my mother. However, there is scriptural basis for divorce in some cases[8] and I found myself in one of those cases. After ten years of marriage, I caught my husband watching homosexual pornography. We hadn't been intimate in over five years at that point; obviously I knew something was wrong, but I was still surprised. Even then, I didn't want to seek a divorce, but, while my husband was back in his home country for a while, his son came clean with me. My stepson told me that my husband of ten years had cheated on me since day one, with both men and women. I believe my husband had really only married me to solidify his legal status in the United States. I felt like I had been scammed. I felt like ten years of my life had been stolen. I started digging and found that everything my stepson told me was true. I discovered every manner of evil and darkness about my husband and realized it was a blessing that he hadn't touched me in five years. I sought the Lord about what I should do. I knew divorce was not only Biblically acceptable in this case, but it was the only real option I had. My second marriage is coming to an end, hopefully more peacefully than my first marriage did. The same pastor who prayed for deliverance cried out to God and declared that these years have not been stolen by the enemy but will be redeemed by the Savior[9]. My mess will be part of His message.

Now I am starting clean, just my younger son and myself, with the Lord and my church supporting me every step of the way. Here I am with no fancy credentials and no legitimate work history, but I know the Lord is with me. I imagine writing a resume, which I haven't done in over twenty years, and putting "kicked out for assaulting a police officer" under education, and "drug dealer, stripper, and unofficial business manager for husband" under work experience. Despite that outward appearance, I walk in victory through my Lord and Savior Jesus Christ. The Lord just continues to amaze me and I continue to persevere in prayer for my family and even for my ex-husbands. I have learned so much from the ladies at church, a group I never would have seen myself spending time with just a few years ago. I have learned about giving and receiving love, about managing anger, about not letting the enemy stifle my voice, and so much more. More than anything, I have felt and experienced the true love of my Savior, both directly in my Spirit and through my church. I believe I'm finally free and about to discover His purpose for the rest of my life. I know He's got me every step of the way.

More to Think About from Ashleigh Grace

Ashleigh Grace's story is full of heartbreak and pain, yet she found deliverance from that pain and now looks to the future with hope. Are you wondering how to find the hope that Ashleigh Grace now has? It's simple, but it's not always easy.

First things first: Do you know Jesus Christ as your Lord and Savior? You may read Ashleigh Grace's story and think that she and some of her family members obviously need a savior. The truth is that everyone needs a savior. Romans 3:23 says all have sinned and fall short of the glory of God. The standard is the perfection of God and all of us, no matter how well we think we've done on our own, fall short of that standard. Romans 6:23 says that the wages of sin is death. It doesn't specify any particular sin or say only the really bad ones; any sin leads to ultimate death and eternal separation from God, and all of us sin. That may sound hopeless, but it's not because God Himself stepped in to save us in the form of Jesus Christ. Romans 5:8 says that God demonstrates His love for us in this: while we were yet sinners, Christ died for us.

What, then, must we do to be saved? Romans 10:9-10 says, "If you declare with your mouth, 'Jesus is Lord,' and believe in your heart that God raised him from the dead, you will be saved. For it is with your heart that you believe and are justified, and it is with your mouth that you profess your faith and are saved." Romans 10:13 says that everyone who calls on the name of the Lord will be saved. This set of verses that the Apostle Paul wrote in the New Testament book of Romans is sometimes called the Romans Road to Salvation[10]. It lays out the why and the how of salvation in plain language.

Right now, wherever you are, you can pray a simple prayer acknowledging that God created heaven and earth and all of the universe; that He exists eternally as the Father, Son, and Holy Spirit; that mankind is sinful and you have sinned against Him; that the Father sent the Son, Jesus Christ, God incarnate, to die for our sins once and for all, raised Him on the third day, and He ascended to sit at the right hand of the Father; and that you want Jesus Christ to be Lord of your life and you want the Holy Spirit to dwell in you. If you sincerely believe in your heart that Jesus died for your sins and rose again and profess with your mouth that Jesus Christ is Lord of your life, you will be saved.

Romans 8:1 tells us that there is now no condemnation for those who are in Christ. With a true faith in Christ, you are assured eternal life with Him.

Like Ashleigh Grace, you can invite Jesus to be Lord of your life and be free from any condemnation. Like Ashleigh Grace, you can pray by the power of the Holy Spirit for deliverance from all that oppresses you, from every evil and adversary, from every sickness and disease, and from your own sinful nature. Everything on earth will not turn out exactly like you hope and all your problems in life won't magically disappear, but you can have spiritual freedom and you can know that God is sovereign. And, like Ashleigh Grace, you can persevere in prayer for your friends and family. Maybe one day you will get to share the Romans Road with someone else.

Prayer verse

Romans 10:12-13 (NIV) For there is no difference between Jew and Gentile—the same Lord is Lord of all and richly blesses all who call on him, for, "Everyone who calls on the name of the Lord will be saved."

Lord Jesus, I have sinned against you and I need you in my life. You are the one true God, Father, Son and Spirit, eternal and almighty. Jesus, you came to earth, died for my sins, and rose again on the third day. Please forgive me and be Lord of my life. Send your helper, the Holy Spirit, to dwell in me …

Just Another Five Years – Whit's Story

"Just another five years." That's what I kept telling myself. High School was about that long. My time in the Marine Corps was about that long. This prison term would be just another five years. One way or another, I could make it through just another five years. The jury had hung three times deliberating a charge of murder. I didn't know what I would do if they hit me with a life sentence for murder. After three tries, the judge told them to consider the lesser charge of reckless manslaughter. They found me guilty on the lowest level manslaughter charge. Twenty split five, the judge said, which meant I would only serve five years in prison and some time on probation. Just another five years, but, little did I know, I would find Jesus Christ in those years.

I have two birthdays. I was born in Cullman, a small city in rural north central Alabama, on April 4, 1977. I was premature, weighing only 4.5 lbs.; my lungs collapsed and they had to fly me to UAB Hospital in Birmingham. That hospital wrote me another birth certificate for April 5th. I was born into a nice upper-middle class family. My dad's parents had emigrated from Ireland and started WC Arnold and Sons Lumber Mill. The family owned 600 acres of timber land which they logged for use at the lumber mill; we still own that land today. We even had the first paintball field in the U.S. on that land, Mt. Doom Paintball in Hanceville, Alabama. I like to say we were all born in the woods, as country as it gets. We weren't wealthy, but the family had done pretty well. Nobody in the family had ever been in serious trouble. I was the first person that I had ever met who got arrested.

I was always pretty athletic. I played serious club soccer around Huntsville, a city in northern Alabama, and ended up being the first freshman to ever play varsity soccer at Cullman High School. Soccer became my anchor; by tenth grade, I already had scouts looking at me. I graduated in 1995 and went on to the University of Alabama at Birmingham. I tore my meniscus in 1996 and got red-shirted for the next year. During that year, I had a bad breakup; within a week, I talked to a recruiter and joined the Marine Corps. I even received an automatic promotion to Private First Class because I had a year of college.

When I joined the Marines, I wanted to be in the infantry. My grandfather had served as an infantry soldier in World War II. My dad was drafted for Vietnam. Instead, he went to Tuscaloosa and played football for Bear Bryant, but, in the end, he joined the reserves and went to Vietnam during the last year of the war. I wanted to be where the action was and became an infantry TOW gunner, part of a unit that hunted tanks.

From there, I went to Surveillance and Target Acquisition and was on the path to become a scout sniper. After a six-month indoctrination and sniper school, I joined a sniper platoon. There were no hazing rules back then and we did all sorts of crazy things to each other, but I loved being a scout sniper. Sniper platoons don't deploy as a platoon: any company in the battalion requests a sniper team and the two-man team deploys with that company. I went to 22 countries as a scout sniper, all during peacetime, mostly for DEA operations, peacekeeping missions, and law enforcement actions. Our special status within the battalion meant we didn't have to follow a lot of the rules and I developed some animosity toward authority as a result. I rose to the rank of Sergeant, E-5, which was the highest I could go in the sniper platoon. At that point, I decided to leave the Marine Corps. I worked out all the time when I was in the military, so I left the service at 6'0", 218 lbs. with 6% body fat. I was a lean, mean fighting machine, a disposition that would be my downfall.

When I re-entered civilian life, I went straight to Florida, where a friend had offered me a job with his dad's construction company. I was only there a few weeks before

JUST ANOTHER FIVE YEARS – WHIT'S STORY

I was recruited to work for the security company Loomis Fargo as an ATM technician. They had a program to rotate between short-staffed branches, so I worked in Florida, Atlanta, and Birmingham, making time-and-a-half plus mileage and meals. After my friend in Florida married, I decided to move back to Birmingham and lived with my brother and another roommate, who would later be my co-defendant.

My brother moved out and eventually married, so it was just my roommate and I living on Birmingham's Southside. He managed a men's clothing store, which meant he dressed well, and he was quite a womanizer. We both went to MMA and Brazilian Jiu-Jitsu gyms. My roommate also had a side gig as a bouncer at a sports bar. We were a couple of roughnecks who liked to fight. I had never been a late night guy, but that changed with a new job I got. I had gotten on the list to buy a Rottweiler from a kennel and made a few trips out to see the dog. I was still working for Loomis at the time, but the lady who had the dog offered me another job and I took it. I became a circulation manager at the *Birmingham News*, the biggest newspaper in the state. It was mostly a daytime job, but I had to go in at midnight some days to make sure deliverers had enough papers. I was responsible for ensuring papers were delivered and for growing distribution in suburban Shelby County, south of Birmingham.

Since this job had me up at midnight, I started going over to the sports bar where my roommate was moonlighting as a bouncer so I could get free drinks. It was only about four blocks from our apartment. He didn't usually drink a whole lot, but, one Friday night, he got plastered. I showed up to the sports bar a little before one in the morning; when he got off at two, we kept drinking. As we walked into the alley behind the sports bar, we were approached by a guy who we thought was homeless asking us for money. It turned out he wasn't homeless, but he was on drugs and mentally ill. There are a lot of beggars around Birmingham and we hated these guys, so we started cussing at him, telling him to get a job. The guy sprayed us with mace and took a swing at my roommate; he jumped on his attacker and we both beat on the guy until I finally pulled my roommate off of him. We walked away from the fight joking about it and still cussing him, as the guy walked away, still cussing us. He had contusions on his face and head from fists and my roommate's elbow. Later, we would learn that he died from blunt force trauma to the head that caused a brain bleed.

The next day, we got a call from the sports bar asking if we knew who had gotten in a fight in the alley. "Yeah, we did," was our reply. Then they told us two detectives were there asking about it because the man had died. He had still been walking around cussing us after the fight; we had no idea we had killed him until that phone call. I talked to my parents, got a lawyer, and then my roommate and I turned ourselves in. That all took place on Saturday afternoon; the detective told us to come in Monday after work. We went back Monday and gave a statement. The detective said he would call if he needed anything else. It didn't even seem like a big deal and I wasn't scared. Three weeks later, detectives came in and arrested me at work in front of my co-workers.

Off I went to jail on $250,000 bond. My grandparents put up the property to bond me out, but my roommate couldn't afford bond. His lawyer told him not to talk to me; eventually we learned that he had taken a plea deal and was going to point the finger at me to try to get a lighter sentence. He sat in jail for months while I was out on bond and still working. Ultimately, I found out on a Friday that my trial would start on the following Monday. My lawyer didn't even get my story until then. My roommate took a twenty-year split sentence and went to prison. I pled not guilty to murder.

I felt like a complete scumbag going into the trial, but I would not plead guilty to murder. Murder required malice and forethought and I had neither in this case. Not guilty was my plea. I got character witnesses, including several fellow Marines. My old battalion commander wrote a letter for me. My family had helped me get an influential Birmingham lawyer, one who would soon become famous in a high-profile political case, but he barely prepared at all. When I went to trial, I had hardly spent any time with him. The trial itself lasted four days. Then the jury deliberated for four days. The jury hung three times; the first two times, the judge sent them back for more deliberation. After they were hung a third time, he directed them to consider a lesser charge of manslaughter. They came back with a verdict of guilty for reckless manslaughter, the lowest possible charge for killing someone.

Suicide was in the back of my mind all of the time. I didn't know how I would survive if I got a long sentence, much less a life sentence. The sentencing hearing was four weeks after they found me guilty of reckless manslaughter. The judge gave me a twenty-year split sentence – I would serve five years in prison. I talked about appealing, but the lawyer said it would be a lot more money and very unlikely to get a better outcome, so I waited at the jail to get sent off to prison, which took close to a year. Five years was manageable. It still seemed unfair: after all, we just beat the guy up. We didn't even know he died. But we could just as easily have run off. It was a choice. We were stupid, we were drunk, and we liked to fight. We made a choice to beat this guy. I probably never would have come to God if this hadn't happened, so, in a strange way, the victim saved our lives.

Violent offenders are held on the ninth floor of the Jefferson County Jail. The jail was kind of like a grain silo, with the officers in the middle surrounded by glass and the inmates in four quadrants around that central shaft. As a violent offender, I had my own cell. There were 24 of us in each of the quadrants. My family couldn't send me any money the first 30 days I was in the jail. The cells had no TV and no radio and we were allowed out only three hours per day for meals. What each cell did have was a white Gideon's Bible[1].

There was a Bible Study on the ninth floor of the jail. I just watched it from the side, but I started reading the Gideon's Bible some out of sheer boredom. After I knew I would only do five years, the thoughts of suicide subsided. Just another five years, I told myself. I mostly tried to keep to myself in jail. I didn't get in to the racial stuff and I didn't play chess and checkers much, though I did make a cardboard chess set and learned a little from some of the inner city guys. A lot of guys in there tried to act tough, but I didn't want anything to do with all of that. I was already in enough trouble because of acting tough and fighting.

My first notes about the Bible were about how stupid it was and how it didn't make sense. I was just smart enough to contradict the "Bible Thumpers" I knew. Growing up I was forced to go to a local church until I was about thirteen. Kung Fu Theater came on at 10:00 am Sunday mornings, so, at age thirteen, I said I wasn't going to church anymore because I'd rather stay home and watch Kung Fu. I went to Vacation Bible School[2] every summer, and, when I was twelve, they made a big push for us to get baptized. I made a profession of faith and was baptized, although I obviously did little to honor that commitment. Still, I know God had His hand on my life from that point on.

The Bible study in jail kept showing me small flashes that made sense. I had always thought only poor, ignorant people believed in the Bible, and the Marine Corps really hardened me in that belief and in other ways, like making killing normal. I would argue with my grandmother about the stupidity of the Bible; I'd say I've been to 22 countries and I'm not ignorant enough to believe that stuff. I read a verse about Jesus chasing the lowly and poor, and it contradicted my view about the South being full of ignorant people simply being deceived by the Bible. There were little glimmers that piqued my interest, but not enough for me to really get involved in the Bible study.

My conversion was a slow one. I had made a thousand promises to God about serving Him for life if He got me out of there. For a while, I wasn't ashamed to go to prayer call, but I wasn't truly a Christian yet either. I didn't want to come to God through a big emotional experience; if I were to come to the Lord, it would be through reason and rational thought. I continued to listen in on the Bible study, reading the Word and studying on my own. Over time, God revealed His truth to me. Before I left the jail for prison, I had gotten on my knees and prayed sincerely for salvation. I had finally given my life to the Lord. And, like me, my former roommate eventually gave his life to the Lord.

After nearly a year in the Jefferson County jail, I was processed in to Kilby Correctional Facility outside of Montgomery, Alabama. Most inmates go to Kilby first and then get shipped out to other prisons in the state, depending on their classification. Kilby was designed for about 1,400 men, but, like every prison in Alabama, it is holding a lot more than that while being staffed by fewer Corrections Officers than it was designed for. Because of my service in the Marine Corps, I managed to get the best institutional job at the facility, which was working in the canteen. It was better than most institutional jobs on its own, but it also meant I got stuff for free all the time. Seeing what got served in the cafeteria, free snacks from the canteen made that the sweetest gig in prison. Kilby had a great chapel staff and the Chaplain wanted me to come be part of the chapel team. That would mean giving up my job at the canteen, so I refused to join the chapel team the entire time I was there. They also wanted me to move to the so-called faith dorm, the safe dorm, but that was where they put a lot of the pedophiles and the crooked law enforcement officers who got caught, so I didn't want to be in there either. Prisons in Alabama have open dormitories with as many as 200 inmates on bunks, not individual or shared cells. So I stayed in my regular dorm instead of the faith dorm and kept my canteen job while I was at Kilby.

My athleticism led to a chance to play on the prison's volleyball team. That was the only real sport we had and it came with some perks. We would actually get taken by bus to play against other prison teams. We had a former high school volleyball coach and a big Samoan who barely spoke English who had played professional beach volleyball. We were really the only organized team in the system. The print shop made trophies that we would send home to our families. Disciplinary action for us was not getting to play volleyball.

My conversion came on my knees at the jail, but I was really sold out for Christ by the time I had been at Kilby for a couple of months. I studied in the chapel library all the time, and, through my studies, confirmed that God is real. I had been a fool my entire life, thinking I was the smart one. It was a spiritual high for two years at Kilby. People called me "Preacher Man" just because they saw me with a Bible. I never actually preached or taught any classes there, not even any exercise yard preaching, the prison equivalent of street preaching. I was generous with the money I got because I believed that was the Christian way to be. Guys would apologize if they cussed around me, which was ironic because I used to cuss like a sailor. Now I cringe if I even hear those words. God delivered me from the desire to cuss right away. I had been chewing tobacco since I had played soccer and that took three years to overcome through the conviction of the Holy Spirit[3].

I had put in for a transfer to be a little closer to my family, but they denied me for a variety of reasons including my job at the canteen and my spot on the prison volleyball team. I thought I would spend the entire five years at Kilby, but, one night, they woke me up and told me I was being transferred. I didn't know where until I got there: Limestone Correctional Facility. Limestone is the largest camp in the state and also quite a bit newer than Kilby; the facility was designed for about 2,000 men, but often houses over 3,000. It was also the safest men's prison in the state while I was there. Limestone is only about 45 minutes from where I grew up, so this was a big improvement for any family members who wanted to visit me. The first thing I did was find the chaplains; there were three and I got along with two of them, but not so much with the third. Unlike Kilby, chapel at Limestone was very inconsistent. Sometimes, the officer at the dorm didn't feel like opening the gate for just a few of us to go to chapel, so we weren't allowed to go. I never told the chaplain about it because of fear of reprisal from the officers.

It was hard to strike a balance as a Christian in prison because I still had to be an inmate too. No guys really bothered me there between my regular weights workout and my martial arts experience. I walked with confidence wherever I went. I got along with the Hispanic inmates because of soccer. My grandmother visited me every two weeks and brought soccer balls that were donated; we even got them to allow cleats for the first time and got those donated from a sporting goods store in my hometown. I got along with the African-American inmates because I worked out with them. I once sent home a picture of me surrounded by my huge workout buddies as a joke that I was in trouble. I got along with the officers because of my experience in the Marine Corps.

When I first transferred to Limestone, someone made a mistake and put me on a farm job outside the fence. My first day out there I saw a prison van flying across the field toward me. They were looking for me but the officer didn't know why. He started asking about my background and what I did in the Corps; when he heard scout sniper, he knew what was wrong. They can't put someone with my background outside the fence on a farm job because I could easily disappear on them. I tried to stay out of trouble and largely out of sight while I did my time. I would see crazy stuff like running knife fights in the dorm, but I stayed out of it and often the officers stayed out of it too. Some of us were big jokers in the dorms. We would push around a wheelchair and try to jump it like a motorcycle. The hobbycraft guys made a jump rope and we would try and throw it to wrap up a guy's legs; I slid to a stop right in front of an officer one day and he just laughed and made me give him the jump rope. We would tie dental floss to a Honey Bun and snatch it away from guys. We were Christians but ran around like the TV show *Jackass*.

I went to Bible Study as often as I could during my time at Limestone and eventually was asked to help teach and lead a Bible Study. I spent three years at Limestone leading worship, doing studies, and really learning the Bible. I started going through Latin, Hebrew, and Greek studies, but a wise man said, "Live it in English first." He told me to pick one verse a day and live it. I would wake up while it was still dark, pray, do a Bible study, and write one verse on a piece of paper. I would pull it out ten times a day and try to live it. I would fold the paper up; once I got up to 25 verses on a sheet of paper, I would mail it home. I could go through the Bible chapter and verse. In some ways, it's easy to be a Christian in prison. When you get back in the free world, a lot of the prayer and study drops off as you get consumed by the cares of the world.

With six months left on my sentence, I got moved to the transition dorm, where you go to a lot of classes that are supposed to prepare you for re-entry into society. This was actually hard for me because it took me away from my job on the weight pile, away from the chapel, and away from my friends. In the transition dorm, I actually started to get scared. I was nervous about getting out. I decided not to be ashamed of my testimony, even though I knew it would take a long time for people and churches on the outside to trust me.

I walked out of prison and already had a good job lined up. A guy I had met rock climbing corresponded with me while I was in prison; I eventually put him on my visitation list and he came to see me every two weeks. He is not a believer, and, as of this writing, I'm still not sure if I was just a curiosity to him or if something drew him to me. He ran a software company and hired me to be part of the quality assurance team. I was not a programmer, but my job was to use the software as a regular user would and try to break it to find any bugs they needed to fix. He already paid me well, but, when he learned he could receive a subsidy for hiring a felon, he gave me a raise and hired a couple of other guys. I worked for him at the software company in Huntsville for a while and even lived in an apartment with my mom for a while when she moved to town. I would go home to Cullman to visit friends and family every weekend. On a trip back to Cullman, I met my wife. I decided to move back to my hometown and leave my software job behind. Eventually, we got married and had two kids. I have a good job, a great family, fun hobbies like rock climbing and racing motorcycles, and ministry opportunities based on everything from my martial arts experience to my prison experience.

Life has gone well for me since I got out of prison, but some parts of Christian life in the free world are hard. It's hard to do in-depth Bible studies between job and family and church responsibilities. For a long time, it was clear that I was only welcome to a certain extent. I was welcome until they realized I knew the Bible better than many of them. I was welcome until it was time to come over to their house. I have to accept that I was in prison and a lot of the church world will have trouble welcoming or accepting me. One great blessing I had after I got out was to volunteer with Kairos Prison Ministry[4]. I'm surprised the warden ever allowed it, but I got to go back to Limestone on Kairos teams and serve the inmates still there. God has used my testimony to bless people there and out here in the free world.

More to Think About from Whit

Like Ashleigh Grace, Whit needed salvation. He needed the healing that comes only from Jesus Christ. And, like so many skeptics today, Whit needed to come to faith rationally, with reason and evidence. Some say there is no evidence for God or the supernatural, but that is patently false. There is tremendous scientific, historical, and philosophical evidence for God; not just for any higher power, but for the one true God of the Bible. The study of facts and reason supporting Christianity is called Apologetics, from the Greek word *apologia*, to make a defense[5]. There are multitudes of apologetics resources, both new and ancient, that can help you understand the facts that support the Bible. It is faith in Christ that saves, but facts and reason help clear away the obstacles that can hinder faith.

One of Whit's favorite resources is a video series called *The Truth Project*[6] from Focus on the Family. Another excellent video series is *Foundations of Apologetics*[7] from Ravi Zacharias International Ministries. There are many excellent books ranging from the C.S. Lewis classic *Mere Christianity*[8] to Lee Strobel's *Case for Christ*[9] to Josh McDowell's *New Evidence that Demands a Verdict*[10] to J. Warner Wallace's *Cold Case Christianity*[11]. What those have in common is that they were written by people who started their studies as atheists. Other highly recommended books include *On Guard*[12] by William Lane Craig, *God's Not Dead*[13] by Rice Brooks, and *Mama Bear Apologetics*[14]. There is really a mountain of evidence for the historical accuracy and validity of the Bible and more books on the subject than most could read in a lifetime. As 1 Peter 3:15 says, always be prepared to give an answer to everyone who asks you to give the reason for the hope that you have. There are solid answers to the claims of the skeptics. And, if you are one of the skeptics, check into these resources with an open mind and you will be surprised how strong the evidence is.

One of the practical things Whit did was meditate on one scripture per day. He wanted to dive off into deep language studies, as many academics tend to do, but godly counsel told him to work on living out the Bible first. He picked one verse per day to meditate on and try to live by example. Meditation is not anything weird: it is just focusing on a particular thing. If you know how to worry, you already know how to meditate. As you read the Bible, certain verses will be especially meaningful to you; these are great ones to pick out and meditate on[15].

Finally, Whit mentioned how Christian life after prison can be difficult sometimes. The truth is Christians are still fallible people and make mistakes. Sometimes the deepest hurts can come from Christians and the church. It is critical to understand that the church is made up of people who have been hurt as well, that they are often still recovering from past hurts or sins, and that they can say or do hurtful things. Church is a bit like a hospital; people are there because they need to get well. There are resources on this topic as well, including Stephen Mansfield's book *Healing Your Church Hurt*[16]. Ultimately, the church is the body of Christ and it is a place of healing and ministry; we are all wounded healers and messy messengers.

Prayer verse

1 Peter 3:15-16 (NIV) But in your hearts revere Christ as Lord. Always be prepared to give an answer to everyone who asks you to give the reason for the hope that you have. But do this with gentleness and respect, keeping a clear

conscience, so that those who speak maliciously against your good behavior in Christ may be ashamed of their slander.

Lord Jesus, I know that You are real and that the Bible is true. Help me to understand You and minister to others as You have called me. Equip me to be a part of your kingdom and your ministry …

Three in Heaven – Tiffany's Story

The first time I went to an abortion clinic, it was quiet. We drove to another state. There were no protesters outside. Nobody in the waiting room said much. It looked like a regular hospital. This time was different. I was only 45 minutes from home. There were people outside, and I just kept my head down as I walked in. There was a girl I knew from high school in there; we agreed not to tell anybody we had seen each other. How could we say we saw someone when it would just incriminate us too? This time, I saw an ultrasound, heard a heartbeat, and started to get attached. I was having second thoughts, but I pushed through it. This time, I felt intense sadness after it was done. This time, I cried all night. This time, I vowed I would never have another abortion. Many years later, I found healing through Jesus Christ.

I was born in Ranson, West Virginia on January 4, 1984. My mother tells me I came in a quick and relatively painless 45 minutes. I am the middle child of three girls. When I was very young, my family moved to Jersey Shore, Pennsylvania, right in the middle of the state, to find work. Dad was a scab, a non-union employee who would cross a picket line, brought in during a union strike at a paper mill.

Mom eventually got a job too, first as a school lunch lady and later at the Overhead Door factory, but she had to lie about her background because she didn't have a high school diploma.

Mom didn't have a high school diploma because she had to drop out and support herself at age seventeen. I never knew him, but her dad was an alcoholic. She used to wake up for school and see her dad passed out in the yard as she walked to the bus. It was a violent home, so much so that her mom once shot at her dad. When she was seventeen, my mom came home from school and her mom was gone. My mom had to quit school and get her own apartment and take a job as a waitress to support herself. The only time she saw her dad after that was when he wandered into her restaurant and asked her for money. Part of my dad's family grew up in foster care because their dad was killed in a hunting accident and their mom committed suicide. Both of my parents tried to do their best, but they didn't have much to work from.

My parents worked hard once they got jobs in Pennsylvania, but they didn't make much money and we survived on a very limited income. Our first house was a foreclosure; there were dead birds inside the windows, the carpets were soaked with urine, and the grass was taller than my little sister. Our second place was a flea-infested trailer.

After that, we got the place where I spent most of my years growing up. It was an old trailer from the 1970s that we fixed up on our own. Growing up, I got two pairs of shoes per year: one when school started and one at Christmas. We only had clothes to last a few days. Eventually I realized that other kids seemed to have different clothes every day of the week, but I'd have to wear the same things at least a couple of times each week.

Early on, I was too naïve to realize the other kids at school were making fun of me, but my older sister remembers being picked on. Once I was old enough to understand, I realized we had less than most of the people we attended school with. I quickly became very insecure about who I was, where we lived, and what I didn't have. Although we had attended church some as a child, I didn't have the security that a real relationship with Jesus creates. Once I became a teenager, I quickly found that security I wanted in the opposite gender. I was the type of girl who always "needed" a boyfriend.

Around the age of fifteen, I began dating and I started to make some serious mistakes. I had already developed a bad habit of stealing when I was in junior high. I had a friend who did it and showed me how to shoplift and get away with it. I didn't have much and I wanted a pair of sneakers so I could run track. I stole some. Once I got away with it the first time, it just kept going and getting bigger. I would go to the mall with friends and we would steal everything and anything we wanted. We made multiple trips in and out of the mall, robbing them of hundreds of dollars' worth of merchandise. I knew that what I was doing was wrong and that I hadn't earned these things, but I cared too much about what other people thought. I didn't have to be the girl who didn't have enough clothes this way. In addition to all the stealing, I began drinking alcohol and smoking cigarettes and exploring sexually with my boyfriends. I would party and drink a couple of times a month, but ultimately my worst issues were rooted in bad relationships. I relied on boyfriends for security.

By age seventeen, my life was crumbling and things were really getting out of control. As a senior in high school, I moved out of my parents' home and into an apartment with my boyfriend. To cope with the stress and instability, I smoked a lot of cigarettes. I was sinking into depression and, although I always kept a job, I skipped school and missed over 70 days my senior year. I'm still uncertain how I was able to graduate. I had experimented sexually with a few previous boyfriends, but this boy was the first one I went all the way with. It turned out he was a cocaine addict.

I found out about the cocaine by accident, soon learning that all of my friends were addicts and that I had been too naïve to realize it. They had all hidden it from me for months. My boyfriend's parents had a big house they had built and had a big extended family that were all over for a cookout one day. I couldn't find him and eventually realized he had been with a group locked in his parents' bedroom. Other times, he would sort of disappear for a while with a buddy, but other friends or girlfriends always covered for him. There were other signs too, like when I would catch him skipping work even though he had a good job. I decided there must be another girl and cornered him. He finally broke down and told me everything. I was so clueless about drugs I had to ask him how cocaine even worked and he explained all about snorting it.

After explaining it all to me, he told me that all of my friends were addicts too. The life I had been living for the past year or more was all a lie. He drove me around this small town pointing out people who did drugs with him and the places they went to get high. I had no idea. My parents had never talked to me about any of these things. It was at that point that I realized I didn't have any true friends and no close relationships with anyone in my family either. During my early teen years, my mom worked second shift so I didn't see her that much; I feel like my dad thought it was my mom's job to talk to the girls. Because of that, it just didn't happen. My dad was so detached he didn't even realize I had a job working on a farm at age fifteen. My younger sister had started using drugs and stealing my stuff, which was part of why I left home and moved in with my boyfriend, yet I was still completely oblivious to my friends' drug use. Here I was at seventeen learning it all from my cocaine addict boyfriend. I was furious and ready to leave him, but he acted like he wanted help with his addiction. He wasn't sincere, but I stayed a while because I thought he was. I even tried marijuana a couple of times because I was angry and decided I would just do drugs too. The second time, I really felt it and drove around high thinking I was speeding when I was really doing about 20mph. Drugs didn't much appeal to me and that was my only experience with it.

We had always been very careful about taking the necessary steps to avoid a pregnancy. When he realized that I would actually leave him if he didn't stop doing drugs, he decided I would stay no matter what if I were pregnant. He sabotaged the measures we had taken and intentionally got me pregnant to keep me with him. I was completely alone, depressed, and pregnant. I didn't tell my parents. I didn't have any friends left to tell. I felt ashamed and helpless. I knew he had done it on purpose so I confronted him and made him pay for an abortion.

We drove all the way to Maryland to an abortion clinic. I was not the first one in the family to make a trip like this. We had gone to pro-life rallies as kids, yet, when my younger sister got pregnant at fifteen, our mom forced her to get an abortion. According to my sister, she didn't want an abortion. As an adult, I challenged my parents about the decision but did not receive any response that I felt justified making my sister have the abortion. Here I was, making the same shameful trip. My sister told me that there had been protesters outside the clinic she went to and that the experience had been really embarrassing, but, when we got to the clinic in Maryland, there was nobody outside the building. It just looked like a hospital. I was relieved there was nobody there because I didn't want to feel guilty. I didn't have any support at all, just the cocaine addict I was forcing to pay for it.

The clinic was clean and the people working there were nice. They didn't do an ultrasound or anything like that. They just had me fill out some paperwork and started me through the process. The whole thing was like an assembly line taking girls through each step one by one. Pay here, wait there, take this pill, go to that room; one after another we went through the steps. I woke up in the recovery room and saw that there were a few other women around. They said everything went fine, gave me some crackers to eat like I had just given blood or something, and told me I would bleed for a couple of days, but, otherwise, they said everything would be fine. I was there for a long time going through the abortion assembly line. I really wasn't sad at the time: I was just glad it was over. I had only been five or six weeks along and went for the abortion the week after I found out I was pregnant.

By the time my high school graduation came in June 2002, that relationship had ended and I was living back at my parents' home without any true friends. My parents didn't know what was going on and I'm certain they didn't understand why I cried during the graduation ceremony instead of celebrating. My life was a mess, I felt utterly alone, and I had absolutely no understanding of my purpose in life. I felt unloved and unwanted, but somehow I continued to press on.

Before long, I found myself in yet another unhealthy relationship. My previous boyfriend had turned out to be a bit of a psycho and had scared off anyone who wanted to be around me. He even crashed his car in front of me on the road one time in an attempt to get me to stop and talk with him. I lived with some amount of fear for years. My new boyfriend fought him off, though, and we didn't waste much time before becoming intimate. He wasn't a drug addict, but neither of us were Christians nor did we act like we were. He said that he was not able to have children, but that was clearly not the case because I was pregnant within a few months. All of these events happened so quickly that, if I hadn't had the first abortion, I would have still been pregnant with my first child when this second pregnancy started.

I once again decided to have an abortion. I still said nothing to my parents. With my first abortion, I felt no sadness or loss afterwards but, with the second one, I felt it. This was the clinic closer to home, the one where I saw a girl from my school. This time, I saw the ultrasound and heard the heartbeat. The father kept saying things like "my baby" and I had to make him stop. I had second thoughts about this abortion, but I made myself go through with it. I cried and cried knowing I had taken the life of an innocent baby. I vowed that I would never have another abortion.

About a year after graduation, in the summer of 2003, I realized that I would never get out of the lifestyle I knew if I didn't go to college. My last relationship fizzled shortly after the abortion and I felt things would never change in my life. I would always struggle unless I did something different. I applied to Lock Haven University, but unfortunately my high school transcripts were so bad that I was not accepted. I lost my job and I was about to be too old to keep health insurance under my parents. I was desperately looking for another job when Sergeant Miller called my parents' home.

Sergeant Miller was an active duty Air Force recruiter. When I answered the phone, she requested some time to sit down and talk. On the phone, she asked me some questions that I don't remember now, but I am sure they had to do with my plans for the future, which I obviously didn't have much of an answer for. I reluctantly allowed her to come and give me her spiel. She provided details about the military; the security in having an income, health insurance, and even continuing education options all seemed appealing. I thought this could be my break. I can join for four years and come back to where I grew up better off. At the time, I had no idea of what God had in store for me.

Without discussing anything with my parents, I enlisted in the Air Force. I found comfort in my recruiter who was a very kind woman that had a similar background. She helped me sign up and get out of the area in an expedited timeframe, approximately one week. I told my parents I had joined the military and I was leaving soon for basic training at Lackland Air Force Base in San Antonio, Texas. At the time, they were not very pleased with my decision. My mom was really mad; I still remember her response, "Do you even realize what you've just done?

You've ruined your life." She didn't even come to my basic training graduation ceremony.

I did okay in basic training and tech school and went on to become a medical technician. My bad habits were still the same and I was still depressed and lonely without Jesus, but I was doing something: I was occupied, employed, and independent. I had new friends that weren't drug addicts and I tried hard to continue to hold my life together. I was really homesick while I was at tech school. My whole plan had been to do four years and go back home. On my wish list of duty locations, every place I listed was in the region I was from. Instead, they said they were sending me to Japan. I literally stood up in class and said, "I can't go to Japan!" when they told me. It didn't matter what I thought though, because that was what the Air Force had decided. After tech school, I went home for two weeks to prepare for my deployment and then headed off to Japan for a two-year assignment.

I arrived in Japan at the beginning of May 2004, and, by the end of the month, I met Alan, the man I would eventually marry. He was just as lost as I was and also just as lonely and depressed, living without a purpose. He had grown up without many good role models. He lived with his mother and stepfather, neither of whom cared much about him, the only child from a previous relationship. Because of his upbringing, he became the type who saw each woman as just another notch in his belt.

I first met Alan at a meeting for the base honor guard. I thought he was cute, but I went around talking to several other people before I approached him because I didn't want to be too obvious. I eventually let him know I was interested and I could see he was thinking, "She's not the right color." The funny thing is the town I grew up in was almost 100% white; Alan was the first African-American man I had ever been attracted to. Growing up, my parents always said everyone was equal, but then they would also repeat stupid stereotypes and jokes. In tech school, I had ended up being friends with some black girls who spent time with me and even rode along with me to the tanning salon. Now here I was interested in a black man and he was the one resistant to an interracial relationship.

Up to this point, I had always required some sort of verbal commitment from my boyfriends before I got involved intimately. Now I see how irrelevant that was, but, at the time, it made me feel like I had some morals and some boundaries. When I met Alan, I threw it all out the window and decided to give the sexually free lifestyle a try. As a result, we started an unhealthy relationship centered on premarital relations that quickly ended in us not talking.

These decisions brought me to the bottom of the barrel once again. I began to do things I would never have done before. I committed adultery by having a relationship with a married man. At one point, I was having relationships with three men at the same time. I was drinking on the weekends and smoking all the time. I had a bad mouth and an attitude you didn't want to cross. I look back now at how ugly I was on the inside and wish I could remember everyone I had ever hurt so I could go back and apologize! I went to clubs and danced in ways women should never dance and I even kissed a female! I was spiraling rapidly out of control and was headed for destruction.

Partying got old quickly for me and I knew what I really wanted was to settle down and be loved. After a few months, I got back in contact with Alan. This time we took things a little slower. I felt peace with him. Neither of us knew Christ but, for some reason, we just seemed more level headed. I stopped partying and smoking shortly after we got back together. Within a couple of months, I was sure I was going to marry him. He still had the mentality that he didn't want to get married or have kids. We had lots of bumps in the road and we still had premarital relations, but, somewhere in it all, we fell in love and became committed to each other.

In June 2005, Alan got orders and left for Hill Air Force Base in Utah. He left me in Japan with no promises of any future together. Two weeks after he got to Utah, he called me and said, "I told my mom that we're getting married." Just like that I made plans to go to Utah for us to get married. On Columbus Day, October 10, 2005, we got married at a courthouse in Farmington, Utah. I had asked my dad to bless our marriage, but he refused because my mom had told him not to do it. Instead, we paid an extra $50 to say vows and had courthouse employees as witnesses. They cried with us like we were their own family. From there, we flew to the East Coast to meet each other's families for the first time. My mom didn't come to a reception my aunt held for us; Alan never even saw my mom.

After the wedding and the brief trip to meet family, I had to go back to Japan for nine months to finish my tour there. Once that tour was over, I was stationed with Alan in Utah, but I had only been there four months when he got deployed to Kuwait. The first year and a half of our marriage, I barely saw him. Fortunately, he worked in the communications shop so he was able to call me all the time.

Once we were finally in Utah together, with Alan's love and support, we both started taking college classes. Alan already had some college credits and I worked hard and took overload classes in order to graduate quickly. Our goal was to have our degrees so we could secure professional careers and separate from the military after our enlistments were completed. During this time, Alan acquiesced on the idea of having children and said that we could have one. We started trying and, within about two or three months, I was pregnant.

Alan was fully aware of my history and, as we started down this road, still without a relationship with Christ, my past began to haunt me. How could I love and desire a child so much now when I absolutely resented one just five years earlier? Why would God bless us with a child after I took the lives of two innocent children? I knew about Jesus, but I didn't really know Him; I had prayed for forgiveness but still didn't have a real relationship with Him. I was about five or six weeks along when I miscarried. It hurt so much. I was scared and thought God really might not allow me to have a baby because of my abortions. Thankfully, before I even had my next cycle, I was pregnant again, and I gave birth to a perfectly healthy baby boy in January 2008.

By this point, I had completed my military enlistment and Alan soon completed his as well. We didn't reenlist because we didn't want to be separated by deployments. Alan graduated with his bachelor's degree in

Management Computer Information Systems while in Utah, and, in 2009, we moved to Woodbridge, Virginia. I finished my degree there and graduated summa cum laude from Park University with a bachelor's degree in Health Care Management. This was huge for me because when I was growing up nobody expected me to go to college. Nobody invested in me. I hadn't even known the difference between an associate's degree and a bachelor's degree. But Alan took the time to invest in me and I graduated with a 3.9 GPA. My only B was at the time that I had the miscarriage.

When our son was eighteen months old, we began to feel the Lord gently tugging on our hearts and we enrolled him in a Christian childcare facility. It had just opened and only had one or two kids; the owners went into debt to open it because they felt the Holy Spirit had called them to it. They started talking to us, and inviting us over for dinner. We continued to feel that tug from the Lord. It was truly the Lord Himself, perhaps because of the prayers of others, that drew us to Him. We decided we should go to church and read the Bible. Alan went to Sam's Club and came home with two New Living Translation Study Bibles[1]. We would read a chapter per night; it was like the Word really was alive. The study Bible helped us understand what we were reading. We would drive an hour to go to the church the daycare owners went to; they became our mentors. It was at their church that we ultimately decided to give our lives entirely to the Lord.

Our son was still a toddler when I became pregnant with a little girl, our only daughter. Things were very tight for us financially. We were low-ranking government civilians in very expensive northern Virginia with an expensive condo, car, and daycare bill. I told our friends we would have to move the kids to a cheaper daycare; the wife cried when I told her and they ended up giving us a huge discount. We were spending three hours per day in the D.C.-area traffic, trying to figure out how we would make it. I was trying to heat pumped milk for my daughter in the car's heater while sitting in traffic when I had my first big revelation from God. "It's not about you," He said. It sounds so basic but it was a revelation. We realized we had built our entire lives around ourselves. We had barely even started reading the Bible, still in the book of Genesis, when we knew it was time for big changes in our lives.

We started applying for jobs all over the world. We said, "Lord, take us wherever you want us, we'll take the first offer we get on faith." We promised Him we would tithe, get rooted in a church, and have our kids in a Christian school. Then Alan got an offer from an agency in Alabama.

All he knew about Alabama was the history of the civil rights era, so his immediate reaction was "I'm not moving to Alabama." I reminded him of our promise to the Lord and our friends advised us to just pray and read the Bible. The first verse we saw that night was about God calling Abraham to leave his homeland. In church that Sunday morning, the preacher talked about the Exodus. It was so obvious that our friends were just staring at us, knowing that word was for us[2]. On Monday, Alan agreed to take the job. The agency only had one job open, nothing for me, and said he had to start within 30 days. There was no money to help us move for this new job, which was a lateral transfer; the government's locality pay system meant he would actually be making less money, albeit in an area with much lower cost of living. We didn't know how we would get out of our expensive condo. In short, we had no idea how we would afford to make this move, but we trusted God.

That week we had $500 show up completely unexpectedly. We used it to take a long weekend trip to Alabama and visit the area over the Martin Luther King Day holiday in January 2012. People were nice to us everywhere we went, which made Alan start to accept that Alabama may not be so bad. We went to the office of the agency Alan would be working for so he could meet the branch chief. He took us into the agency director's office, with all of the branch chiefs there; our kids were running around the office while we met with all of the agency leadership. It was a weird meeting because they kept asking me a lot of questions as I was chasing the kids around. At the end, I figured out why: they offered me a job too. In fact, they created a position just for me!

I spoke with a realtor so that we could look at houses on that trip. We looked at a few on our list, but we knew immediately that the first one we saw was for us. We made an offer on faith since we had no idea how we would pay for it, signing a contract the Saturday of our weekend trip. Before this trip, I had researched churches and Christian schools; we went to a school and immediately knew that was the place. We went to their church on Sunday morning and just cried and cried because we were so touched by the Holy Spirit while we were there. We knew we were home.

When we returned to Virginia, we received a huge five-figure tax refund that was totally unexpected. That money paid for everything we needed to move and get into the house we had under contract. Our condo rented right away and stayed rented for two years until we finally sold it. God miraculously met every need that had seemed so impossible for us. We made our move to Huntsville, Alabama, and were baptized in the church we fell in love with on Easter Sunday 2012.

THREE IN HEAVEN – TIFFANY'S STORY

The Lord eventually led us to move to a smaller house, where I would homeschool my children and have an impact on other kids in the neighborhood. In addition to my three in heaven, God is allowing me to raise five amazing children, four boys and one girl, with another baby on the way as of this writing. He also allows me to interact with a lot of the kids around us, a chance to invest in them the way I wish someone had invested in me at that age. We have peace and joy and, most of all, love. My life is better and more fulfilling now than I could have ever dreamed or imagined myself. I have stability and security in Him. My children only know of His love and our love for them. Jesus can do amazing things when we hand Him something broken. I am far from perfect, but He carries me. He helps me through and He is always there. He never fails me.

When I look back now, I see how the Lord was working in my life even though I hadn't invited Him in. I tried to fit numerous puzzle pieces into the hole I had inside. The only piece that fits is Jesus. His love is all I ever needed and ultimately He was there helping me get through, leading me to the military, to Alan, and ultimately to Himself. Isaiah 61:3 says "He will give a crown of beauty for ashes, a joyous blessing instead of mourning, and festive praise instead of despair." The Lord is true to His word and He miraculously turned my life around.

More to Think About from Tiffany

By the grace of God, Tiffany has overcome her difficult past and now lives in joy and hope with the love of Christ Jesus. Many of us have things in our past that we are not proud of, things that haunt us, and things that the enemy likes to remind us of and use to knock us off course. As the popular saying goes, when the enemy reminds you of your past, remind him of his future! 1 John 1:9 tells us if we confess our sins, God is faithful and just and will forgive us our sins and purify us from all unrighteousness.

The apostle Paul told us one thing he does is forget what is behind and strain toward what is ahead[3], and he certainly had a lot in his past to leave behind! Before he met Jesus, Paul had participated in the stoning death of Stephen, the first Christian martyr, and actively persecuted the church all over the region[4]. Despite this, God transformed Paul into arguably the most influential of the disciples, responsible for writing a huge portion of the New Testament. In the Old Testament, it was King David, who God called a man after His own heart, who was guilty of adultery and murder[5]. When we repent and seek God sincerely, He can transform us and use us in mighty ways!

Tiffany overcame her situation and her past by diligently reading scripture, by being obedient to the Holy Spirit, and by remaining steadfast in prayer. Spending time

THREE IN HEAVEN – TIFFANY'S STORY

with the Lord and reading the one and only truth is always the best resource to help where you struggle. There are also numerous great resources on the subject of overcoming your past, like the *Unstuck* series by Chip Ingram[6], *Overcomer* by David Jeremiah[7], and *It's Not Supposed to Be This Way* by Lysa Terkeurst[8]. If there is a single theme of the entire Bible, it is redemption. The story of redemption ties everything together. That redemption is available to every one of us if we trust in Him!

And if you or someone you know is in the specific situation Tiffany was in, with an unplanned pregnancy, there is help in the form of Crisis Pregnancy Centers[9] and organizations like Heartbeat International[10]. These are places you can go to get real help, without judgment, completely free of cost. No matter what you have done or what situation you are in, God loves you and His grace is more than big enough for you.

Prayer verse

Ephesians 1:7 (NIV) In him we have redemption through his blood, the forgiveness of sins, in accordance with the riches of God's grace.

Lord Jesus, You know that I have sinned and that my past still haunts me despite the assurance of your forgiveness. I know that You can redeem me and my past. I pray for your grace that I may accept your love and forgiveness and the future You have for me ...

Rock and a Hard Place – Barry's Story

My last night as a crack addict I drove to my usual spot to get high. When we finished, my car wouldn't start. The car was the last thing I still had in my life at that point and now it didn't even work for me. Eventually I made it home and climbed in bed; by 3:00 am I was crying uncontrollably. I didn't know how to pray so I just cried out, "God take this from me, I can't quit!" The next day, I was riding a mountain bike down the shoulder of the highway with one crack rock and one piece of crack stem on me. I rode behind an oil change place and saw an old bus and a desk back there. I put the rock and the stem on that desk and flicked the rock off onto the ground. Five seconds later, I was on my hands and knees on the pavement looking for that rock, wondering what I had just done. After half an hour, I realized I wasn't going to find it. I rode home through the projects and found a guy who had some crack, but he lived two towns over. I had the stem and he had rocks at home, so he got on the handlebars of my bike and we started the ten-mile ride to his house where we could get high. By then, it was dark and we got pulled over for riding a bike at night with no light. I had been driving my car around for weeks with no tag, no license, and no insurance, and with a shotgun that was registered to somebody else in the trunk. But now, on a bicycle with another crack addict on the handlebars, I got pulled over. I didn't know it then, but God was looking out for me. After one night in jail, I was able to go home. Rock bottom was riding a bike ten miles to get a rock to smoke.

My parents were both crystal meth addicts when they were raising my sisters and me. When I look back, I don't really see drug addicts as parents; I remember some fairly normal times growing up. My older sister remembers making a place to hide our parents' drugs in case the cops raided our house. She stayed awake worrying about the police coming and taking our parents away. My mom remembers me almost shining a public light on her addiction when, sitting in a high-chair at McDonald's, I was sticking a straw up my nose just like I had seen her do. Now I know a lot more about what my parents went through.

Though they were functioning addicts, my parents were loving, taking care of us and putting food on the table. We lived in poverty, but that could have been avoided if they hadn't squandered everything. Since they were living as addicts, they didn't discipline us. From a young age, we wandered the neighborhood and did whatever we wanted with no consequences. Even when the police brought me home for things like digging up street signs and throwing rocks at cars, my parents didn't really care.

We lived in the same house from the time I was born until I was about twelve years old. That's when my parents divorced. My mom and my middle sister moved into my uncle's house, which was eight hours away by car. All three of us had wanted to stay where we grew up, which meant staying with my dad, but my middle sister had started getting in trouble and dad said he couldn't handle her. Mom moving away brought abandonment and codependency issues into my life. I went through the stages of grief when they left, which made a huge impact on me. I started experimenting with drugs for the first time. I got high with some of the neighborhood kids and I drank and smoked at home. Around the same time, I discovered pornography and developed an unhealthy view of women. All of this mixed together to create a destructive state of mind for me. My mom and middle sister moved back much closer to me after about a year, but the damage was done.

When it was just my older sister, my dad, and me, he really started to act out, getting drunk with the neighbor across the street who was also recently divorced. We were thirteen and filling cups for him and drinking ourselves. When my mom moved back, she lived with my grandparents for a while, before eventually meeting my stepdad and moving in with him. He drank alcohol but didn't do drugs. About halfway through my freshman year of high school, I moved in with my mom, my stepdad, and my sister, who by then had a son of her own. My mom had stopped doing drugs but wasn't saved yet; she was seeking forgiveness and acceptance in all the wrong ways. She would drink and smoke cigarettes with us and I would basically get wasted with my mom.

Because there was not much discipline from my mom or dad, the kids did some crazy stuff. One night I got high with some friends and we decided to hop on a train and ride a mile to the convenience store. We were running on top of the train cars and I fell through a big hole in the roof of one car. That car had been hauling manure, its bottom still covered in an inch-thick layer. I got knocked out when I landed and rolled around in manure for a while. When I woke up, I was stuck, which meant I had to spend the whole night in there. The next morning, it took the Conrail Police and two fire trucks to get me out at the train yard. The train ended up pretty close to my mom's house so my sister came and picked me up. There were times I'd go to parties and get so drunk that I'd fall asleep in my own vomit. My dad didn't seem too concerned with where I was or who I was with as long as I made up any reasonable excuse for not coming home. I lost my virginity to my first real girlfriend by the time I was sixteen years old. She slept over at my house and nobody ever even knew about it. She just told her mom and dad that she was sleeping over at a friend's house.

I joined the Navy after high school. I went in with my sister on the same weekend; we even ended up on the same ship. I did well in the military with the structure and discipline I never had growing up[1]. I didn't do drugs since I was working as a cryptologist with a very high level security clearance, but I definitely drank and partied a lot. I was a good sailor, but you don't have to be a Christian to be a good sailor. Even then, I felt like God had a calling for me, but I didn't have a church background and nothing I did to try to fulfill that calling ever lasted. My mom got saved around the time I got out of the Navy. My grandparents were true Jesus Freaks and my mom had heard about the Teen Challenge[2] program growing up. Unlike most people who go to Teen Challenge to get sober, my mom got sober and then started volunteering at Teen Challenge.

I went to Tijuana, Mexico for my nineteenth birthday and got blackout drunk while bar-hopping one night. As I was leaving the bar, my friend and I were lured into a back alleyway where we ended up paying for two Mexican prostitutes. I was too drunk to even do anything, but it was a serious compromise of what I knew was wrong at the time, even without any real church upbringing. During my first six-month deployment, when my ship was in port in Phuket, Thailand, I got so drunk that I almost missed the liberty boat on our last night in port. I was about five minutes from missing the ship and being left in Thailand by myself. I was twenty at the time. I also had my second and only other experience with a prostitute while in port there.

I was at sea during Operation Iraqi Freedom. At the end of my tour, we had been at sea 99 days. To get home, I took a helicopter to Bahrain and then a flight to San Diego, where I was discharged. It was when I left the Navy that I went off the deep end doing drugs and partying like crazy. Now a civilian, I was living in Washington, D.C. I started smoking pot and then I started selling it to support my habit. I also had gotten married, but I started cheating on my first wife all the time. It didn't take long to go from pot-smoker to full-blown crackhead. For four years, I lived a double life trying to hold a job during the day and living as a drug addict at night. I eventually left my wife, completely crushing her because she had no idea that my life was quietly and secretly spiraling out of control. After we separated, I spent the next several years living with different people, sleeping on couches and rooming with people I barely knew. It all sort of came to a crescendo when I eventually moved into a small two-bedroom apartment with three other men. The plan was for me to sell pot to pay my share of the rent, while another roommate sold crack, and another sold cocaine. I had nothing left of my personal belongings by this point except for the clothes on my back and a queen-size mattress on the floor. I can remember many sleepless nights just waiting for someone to break in and rob us for our drugs or for the police to break in and arrest us, but the time never came.

I hated my life, but I couldn't stop; it was like crack was the driving force behind everything I did. Crack causes a chemical reaction in your brain the first time you do it. You never quite get that same reaction again, but you keep looking for it. My life fell apart. After our separation, I got divorced from my first wife. I couldn't hold a job. I went from having my own place in D.C. and working great jobs at the State Department and the Defense Intelligence Agency to moving in with my mom and working as a waiter at a chain restaurant three years later. Mom felt obligated to help me; she wouldn't kick me out because she had been an addict raising me.

After I moved back in with my mom, I met some people in the projects who taught me how to cook my own crack from cocaine. I spent my nights just getting high. Before my car got repossessed, I used to rent my car out to the dealer for crack. He would give me a huge ball of crack as "rent" to use my car to make drops in. I would call the guy every couple of hours and ask him for more because I ran out of what he gave me. I started stealing stuff from my parents and pawning it. I would steal their stuff, get some cash for it, go to the projects, and get crack. The only place I didn't feel paranoid smoking crack was at the cemetery beside my grandmother's grave. I was depraved enough to think doing it there would keep me from getting busted.

When I moved back in with my mom, I really wanted to stop doing drugs, but I couldn't. I was a hoodlum and was arrested a couple of times for possession. The conviction of God really started to hit me. I knew my mom was staying up all night praying for me. She would often try to wait up for me to come home and I would sit on the porch until she went to bed just so I didn't have to face her. On Thanksgiving, my mom and stepdad took me to Teen Challenge, an intensive Christian rehabilitation program, to help them cook Thanksgiving dinner for the men there. I started hearing testimonies from guys that had been just like me a few weeks before. I told my mom I wanted to go to Teen Challenge, but I kept procrastinating about doing it.

One night after that, I came home, and waited for my mom to go to bed before I came in and crawled in bed myself. I was completely broken. I poured my heart out to the Lord. I didn't grow up in church and didn't know how to pray, so I just cried out to God. The next day, I drove my car with a few of my "smoke buddies" to our usual spot, a playground in the projects where we would sit and get high. After we ran out of crack to smoke, my car wouldn't start. This was the beginning of a series of events which I now realize is how the Lord chose to answer my cries for help the night before. Having my car break down did not slow my addiction any as I rode my bicycle from town-to-town the next day still managing to pawn things for drug money. As I rode my bicycle through the projects at midnight the day after I abandoned my car at that park, I got pulled over by the police and arrested. The beautiful mercy of this story is the fact that just one day earlier, I was driving a car around with expired tags, a suspended license, countless bags of drugs in the glove box, and an improperly registered firearm in my trunk – the same way I'd been getting around for months up until that point. On this night, however, the police pulled me over for what he explained was "riding a bike at night without a light." I had a bag of weed and a crack stem on me at the time, still much better than all the illegal activity I could have been guilty of just a night prior. I got out of jail the next day, went home, and confessed everything to my parents. By the grace of God, the staff at Teen Challenge let me enter the program the next day. This is when the good part of life started.

ROCK AND A HARD PLACE – BARRY'S STORY

My temptation to smoke crack was instantly gone when I started Teen Challenge. When I walked through the doors, I was so run down from drug use I could barely walk. I used a softball bat as a cane to help me get around. I was so malnourished I had toenails just fall off. The rules at Teen Challenge are very strict and I was convinced the center in Philadelphia had it out for me. A couple of weeks in, I broke the rules to go to a pay phone and call my mom. They wouldn't let me back in the center when I came back. She got me a ticket to San Diego and I started again at Teen Challenge Southern California.

The first month, as I was trying to recover from the physical devastation of drug abuse and malnourishment, I would wake up in agony with back pain and tight calves around 3:00 am every night. Guys would pray and help me stretch out every day until one day I woke up with no pain at all. I had received miraculous healing and my body weight began returning to a normal, healthy level as well. I was finally healed physically and began to praise God in the shower one morning; that's when I was filled with the Holy Spirit[3]. After graduating the program, I worked at the Pittsburgh Teen Challenge for six months because I did not trust myself to leave the program. I got out in 2008, after nearly two years of faith-centered rehabilitation.

I started out working a low-wage job and living with my dad in North Carolina. I moved back to the D.C. area on faith and got a job with an IT company doing a contract for the Social Security Administration. That led to a contract to replace computers at a larger contractor. I would carry the old "Million Dollar Gospel" tracts[4] that looked like money. I was replacing a computer for the company's vice president when he saw me and said, "Hey, you have some money hanging out of your front pocket." That led me to share my whole testimony with him. When he found out I had been a cryptologist in the Navy, he had their Human Resources department call me with a job offer. They checked and found that my security clearance was still good and had exactly three days before it expired. They hired me in two days so they could sponsor me to keep the clearance. God truly provided that opportunity for me at just the right time.

While I was going through Teen Challenge in California, my mom was volunteering at the Teen Challenge in Philadelphia and met a young woman in the program who had been through a lot of her own struggles. I had been in Teen Challenge for almost two whole years, unable to strike up a relationship because of their strict rules about talking to women. After I finished my time in Teen Challenge, I was living and working with my father in North Carolina and I was beginning to really want to talk to a girl.

It was as if I had forgotten how to approach a woman because I had been forbidden to for so long. The idea intimidated me. I would tell my mom everything at that time and I remember telling her things like "I just want to have a conversation with a girl." She used to make little jokes about how she met a nice girl who she thought would be great for me, so one time I actually pursued it. On one of our usual phone calls, as I was expressing how badly I wanted to just have a woman to talk to, let alone take out on a date, my mom made the comment, "I met your future wife today." I asked my mom to ask that girl if I could give her a call. She lived in Maryland with her father at the time and I was in North Carolina with my father. We were both fairly recently graduated from Teen Challenge. When we spoke for the first time, I felt a very strong connection with her. That young woman, Lauren, is now my wife.

God blessed us through a couple of job changes while we were in the D.C. area, and the birth of our first child, Abigail. She had a very difficult delivery, which required immediate surgery, and still has continuing health and developmental problems. I was working a job making entry-level money at the time. It was a great job compared to the odd jobs making minimum wage that I had been doing to get by after graduating from Teen Challenge, but it wasn't going to be enough to support a family. When we found out Lauren was pregnant with Abigail, I began sending out my resume; I was eventually offered a job working for the FBI Academy in Quantico, VA. They were going to pay me enough money to support my small, growing family. The best part was it was a salaried position with full benefits so Lauren could stay home with the baby. I waited to get an offer letter for this position before putting in my two-week notice at my other job. It was going to work out perfectly; Lauren was scheduled to be induced into labor so we actually knew the date Abigail was going to be born. I worked it out that I would have two weeks off after leaving my current job before starting my new job with the FBI, which meant I could spend those two weeks with Lauren and Abigail. We even moved into a nicer apartment in a nicer part of town, closer to Quantico. As we were dealing with all the unknowns about Abigail's health, we had to stay at a Ronald McDonald house near the Washington D.C. Children's Hospital. Knowing that I'd be starting this great new career opportunity with full benefits gave me some measure of peace. However, as I was in the hospital with Lauren and Abigail, on the Friday before my start date, I got a call from the new job. They told me that my prior arrest record meant the FBI would not give me access to Quantico, so they had to withdraw the job offer!

When it seemed like the last shred of hope I had was pulled out from under me, my training that I received in Teen Challenge kicked in. I didn't panic or fret; God gave me an unexplainable peace[5]. While everyone in my life was telling me to hire an attorney and sue the company, to "give them a piece of your mind," I leaned into Jesus. I shut the door of our hospital room while Lauren and Abigail were in the NICU and I dropped to my knees. "God, you have always proven yourself faithful. I know that there is a reason this job didn't work out, but I don't understand why all of this is happening. You are my provider, Lord, so please do what you do best and open another door for us." Within a week, I had another job offer that was even better than the one with the FBI Academy! If I hadn't been forced into a different job, my career would never be where it is today because it was eventually through that position that I received the opportunity to become a civil servant. Throughout these struggles, God has been faithful.

God eventually led us to Huntsville, Alabama, where our second daughter, Emma, was born. When deciding on the move, I fasted for three days and we prayed for three things: We didn't want to go through a long time searching for a church like we had in a previous move, we wanted good Christian fellowship with couples our age, and we wanted wisdom looking for a house. We visited a couple of churches that weren't quite right for us. I had sent an email to a lot of churches in Huntsville asking what they believed about the gifts of the Spirit and I got a reply from one that was all about believing in the fullness of the Spirit and not limiting God. We visited, and, in the first ten minutes, we knew this was the church God had for us. He answered two of our prayers at once with that, answering the third not long after.

When I first walked into Teen Challenge, I was instantly delivered from substance abuse and addiction. My addiction to pornography and my unhealthy view of women were not as easily broken. While I was in Alabama, my pornography addiction nearly cost me my security clearance and my job, which had a predictable impact on my marriage. Eventually, we decided to move back to New Jersey; in Alabama, the law did not require insurance to cover the therapy Abigail needed, but, in New Jersey, it did. My employer was able to assist me with a transfer, so we moved back to my home where my mom could help us and the insurance would cover more of our needs.

The transition back was more difficult than we expected. We weren't there long before Lauren was pregnant, but we were crushed when she miscarried. She fell back into some of her own struggles with addiction and self-harm after this. I still struggled with sexual impurity. We both continued in Celebrate Recovery[6], a Christian recovery and support program, as we struggled to stay clean. In my struggle with lust, I would gain and then lose ground, but I was never done.

After a couple of years, I hit a point where I was simultaneously fighting my battle with lust and the biggest battle of my marriage as our relationship problems continued to grow. We were in counselling and hit the point of talking about separation; I was asking friends if I could sleep on their couches. My Celebrate Recovery sponsor told me, "She wants you to respond by fighting for her heart." This is the same mentor who had been trying for over a year to help me understand the finished work of the cross. I had been reading Watchman Nee's *The Normal Christian Life*[7], and, for months, I was pleading with God, "Please help me to see her as You see her, and to love her the way that You love her." It seemed that the more I prayed this way, and the more I tried to make our relationship better, the more distance grew between us. It was beginning to feel hopeless.

Then one day, I read an illustration in Nee's book, in which a younger believer and an older believer are having a conversation and the younger believer is explaining how hard he's been trying to overcome a particular sin in his life. He explains that it seems like the harder he tries, the more prevalent the sin becomes, and the further he seems to grow from looking more like Jesus in his life. The more seasoned believer places a coffee cup on the table and asks the struggling believer to imagine that this coffee cup could pray. He goes on to express how crazy the cup would sound begging and pleading with God to give it the ability to hold coffee and keep it hot and make coffee transportable for the person drinking it. It's already a coffee cup! That's when the image of Jesus' finished work on the cross finally made sense to me. For ten years as a Christian, I thought I had to work to become more like Jesus all on my own. That's why I had been pleading for Him to make me more like Him. The truth is that Jesus took my sin and he carried my sinful nature to the cross with Him. I was crucified with Christ the moment I put my faith in Him.

As crazy as it is for a coffee cup to beg God to make it a coffee cup, it's just as crazy for a follower of Jesus to beg and plead with God to make them more like Jesus! It's just as crazy for a Christian to work to become more like Jesus. That work was already done for us! We just have to walk out our salvation with fear and trembling[8], as Paul said. It was at that moment that I began to change my perspective. Instead of trying to fix my marriage and begging God to help me love my wife like He does, I began to surrender it to God and trust that all the work was already finished. "God, I have been trying to fix my marriage, but I can't. I don't have that ability. Only You can do that. Please, give me more faith to believe that I died to myself, and it is no longer I who live, but You who lives in and through me. Give me more faith to believe that I have your eyes to see my wife, and I have your heart to love her." It seemed instant. My marriage was restored and I suddenly had my best friend back! I didn't do anything in my own strength. I just trusted in the work that was already done for me, the finished work of the cross.

I am justified and sanctified through Christ; when Jesus said, "It is finished[9]," it was all finished right then. My prayer for my wife became, "God give me the faith to know I already have the ability through Christ to love her as You love her." Within a week of this epiphany and changing the way I prayed, there was a 180-degree turnaround in my marriage. Healing came from God, His grace was sufficient, and it changed everything in my recovery and purity. I am making more progress and living in more victory and the fruit is evident in my marriage. God has been faithful throughout my life, protecting me as I grew up, saving me from myself on so many occasions, and finally bringing me to the full realization of how amazing His grace really is.

More to Think About from Barry

Barry's downward spiral into substance abuse is an altogether too common story in the United States today. His life got worse and worse until he hit rock bottom; often hitting rock bottom is what has to happen for an addict to finally seek help. Not allowing an addict to hit rock bottom can be an act of enablement. After Barry hit rock bottom, he found healing in Teen Challenge, a year-long intensive residential program for young people who struggle with addiction. The story of Teen Challenge is told in the David Wilkerson classic, *The Cross and the Switchblade*[10]. Teen Challenge centers can now be found in almost every part of the world. If you or someone you know is struggling with addiction, there may be a Teen Challenge center or similar Christian ministry that can help them overcome addiction through the power of the Holy Spirit in their area.

The power of the Holy Spirit is a central tenet at Teen Challenge and similar programs. The Spirit is a part of God that is sent to dwell in us when we accept Jesus Christ as Lord and Savior. We can then truly allow the Holy Spirit to manifest in us and allow us to experience many of the gifts described throughout the New Testament. The Holy Spirit will lead us and guide us if we train ourselves to hear his voice through prayer and reading the Bible[11].

Barry also experienced a series of events after he gave his life to Jesus that helped him step from one place God called him to the next. Sometimes it seemed like he was at a dead end, sometimes it seemed like the rug was pulled out from under him, and sometimes he wasn't really sure what to do next. God often uses circumstances and seasons in our lives to act as bridges from one thing to the next; if He tried to take us straight from step one to step twenty without these bridges between, we might never take a step at all. God can use every circumstance and setback to prepare us for what He has in store for us next.

Years after Barry had overcome substance abuse, he was still struggling with other issues in his life. He was reading *The Normal Christian Life*, a classic by Watchman Nee, and working with a Christian mentor when he had an epiphany about the finished work of the cross. When Jesus said "It is finished" from the cross, He meant it was all finished. As believers we are able to live in victory in every area of our lives, not through our own power but through faith in His power dwelling in us. The Apostle Paul told us that He who began a good work in you will perfect it until the day of Christ Jesus, and that, in Him, you have been made complete[12]. We just have to accept His grace!

Prayer verse

Philippians 2:12-13 (NIV) Therefore, my dear friends, as you have always obeyed—not only in my presence, but now much more in my absence—continue to work out your salvation with fear and trembling, for it is God who works in you to will and to act in order to fulfill his good purpose.

TESTIMONIES OF GRACE

Lord Jesus, I know that by your grace alone I am saved. Your finished work on the cross allows me to live in victory, if I would only believe. Lord, give me the grace to understand that I already have inside me the same power that raised You from the grave ...

Scars on Her Heart – Lauren's Story

The cutting isolated me. Right after I cut myself, it felt good, but I wouldn't want anyone to see me until it healed. Then I was alone and that made me want to do it again; it became a cycle, just like the drugs. While my mom was sick, I would look after her during the day and do drugs at night. When she passed away, I didn't care about anything anymore and all of those problems only got worse. My dad eventually got sick of me and kicked me out after I stole a lot of money from him. With my mom gone and my dad done with dealing with me, I hit rock bottom. Sometimes rock bottom is part of the path to finding Jesus.

My mom was a real fighter when she was young. I didn't know just how much of a fighter she was until long after she was gone. Before she became pregnant with me, she went to the hospital for what should have been a routine gall bladder surgery. One thing after another went wrong, so they opened her up several times trying to figure out just what was happening. She was diagnosed with a blood fungus and transferred to one of the best hospitals in the country for more surgery and treatment. At one point, the doctors didn't even sew her back up; they just left her belly open from end to end. She was on so much medication that my dad thought she was hallucinating when she said they hadn't sewn her up, but it was true. Eventually, the doctors said they were going to close her up and let her die because there was nothing else they could do. They brought in clergy to comfort her.

Her father was there with her the whole time. He told them she was a fighter and that she was not going to die. He was right. She was in the hospital for months, but, after they closed her up and took her off most of the medication, she slowly started to get better. Just a few months after her recovery, she became pregnant with me. The doctors, her friends, and some family members said she should get an abortion. Her body had been through so much; she had been on so many medications that surely something would go wrong with one or both of us. She refused to even consider it. The doctors were wrong again: I was born healthy and she lived many more years. We had a special bond from the beginning. She had scars from her sternum to her pelvis from the exploratory surgeries and big scars from the drainage tubes. She used to joke about all of the scars. She was so strong and determined back then.

My feelings of depression started when I was fourteen. I got upset all the time and I didn't know why. I didn't know it was depression, but I definitely thought something was wrong with me. I would make mix tapes of sad songs. I would go to the nearby community beach at night and just cry and cry by myself. I was shy and anxious about going to school, so I would get there and start crying and my parents would come get me. They would leave me at home while they worked and I would cry all day at home. I missed so much school that I wasn't sure I was going to graduate.

I was fifteen the first time I smoked cigarettes and drank alcohol. I never told my dad anything and I wasn't as close with my mom in those years. When I drank, I felt better, which made me want to do it more. I had grown up saying I would never drink or smoke or do drugs; every new thing I tried was something I said I would never do. I very quickly went from smoking a cigarette to shooting up hard drugs. When the feelings of depression started at fourteen, I didn't know what to do. At fifteen, I discovered drugs made me feel better, but it wasn't a permanent fix.

My mom and dad divorced when I was young, but later got back together. They raised my older sister and me; we had all the material things we needed but there was no affection, no loving touch, nobody saying "I love you." My dad always seemed angry and resentful, like he was just bothered by us all the time. He would often get right in our faces screaming at us; he even got physical a couple of times. One time, he shoved me down and said, "Go to your room and cry like a baby." I did, but I realized that I could turn it off and not feel anything. This was the start of my defense mechanism of not showing any emotion at all.

I didn't know what depression was when I was a teenager; I just knew there were powerful feelings that I couldn't seem to overcome. I didn't tell anyone what I was feeling. I lost two people who were very dear to me during my teenage years. One was my grandfather. I didn't cry in front of anybody no matter how much grief I felt for him. This defense mechanism was fully engaged by then. I just started shutting down; my dad didn't want drama and, if I didn't show any emotion, maybe I wouldn't feel any emotion either. No emotion would be better than the feelings of depression.

The other person I lost was my mom's brother; she loved him and I shared a birthday with him. He was in the Navy and an amazing architect. He had lived with AIDS for years but finally succumbed to the disease. I saw him a couple of days before he died and he looked like nothing but a skeleton. This only added to the deep feelings of depression that I was trying to hide. After my uncle died, the substance abuse and suicidal thoughts only got worse.

I was one of the only people in my group of friends who had access to a car. I actually totaled a car on an icy road a month after I got my license, but I was sober that time. After that, I made it through the rest of high school without destroying any more cars, which was miraculous given how often I drove high. Since I had my parents' car, I drove a lot, and would cram a ridiculous number of people in the car. They would be sitting on each other's' laps or even in the trunk. I started dropping acid my junior year and would drive my friends around while hallucinating from the LSD. One time, it started snowing and I actually thought I was playing a video game. I was just careless and didn't value my life and did dangerous stuff all the time.

By my junior year, my mom had gotten sick and was diagnosed with Hepatitis C. I became one of the caretakers for her, cleaning up after her and making sure she was safe while she drank. She kept drinking more and more despite having a liver disease. In my senior year of high school, I was at a friend's house with a group of people and didn't want to be there anymore. I locked myself in the bathroom and tried to kill myself. My boyfriend broke the door down to get me out. The day after I tried to kill myself, two friends told my mom so she took me to a therapist. This started years and years of doctors and diagnoses of things like anxiety and manic depression. I tried a lot of different medicines, but they didn't make me feel any better. Only the illegal drugs made me feel better. I tried to commit suicide a couple more times, even using the sleeping pills prescribed by my therapist in a suicide attempt. I would have preferred to go to sleep and never wake up than keep living with the pain I felt. I would write a note and take so many sleeping pills, but I would still wake up; once I woke up because my dad was getting me up to take care of my mom. I remember waking up for school after one of these attempts and having so much medication in me that I couldn't even walk straight trying to go to the bus stop. When I got to school, I fell asleep all day. Amazingly, I did finally graduate high school in 1996.

In high school, I had fallen in love with dance. I had a dance teacher I loved and looked up to, but she was a lesbian. This led to a struggle with my sexuality and same-sex attraction. This struggle only added to the cocktail of feelings that bubbled inside me. The dance classes I took as a teenager also weighed us periodically and, no matter how skinny I was, I always had poor body image. I started taking laxatives and using it as sort of a reverse bulimia. I was never diagnosed with an eating disorder, but I still struggle with food even today. So many negative things in me grew roots in high school and spiraled out of control for years.

In 1997, I moved to California to pursue my dream of dancing. I had gone out there a couple of summers before that and stayed with my dance teacher while I was there. Right after I graduated high school, my mom had decided to leave my dad and move to California, so I joined her and stayed with her. I think she basically waited for me to be out of high school before she left. My plan was to work for a year and save money before I went. When I got there, I got a job at a toy store and immediately found people to smoke weed with. In the end, I only ever went to one dance class and to one audition for extras that didn't work out.

While I was in California with my mom, she started telling me everything bad about my family. She told me about how my dad had cheated on her multiple times, which made me hate him even more. She told me things about my beloved grandfather that I wish I had never heard. While I was with her in California, she drank with me and let me smoke weed in her apartment. We grew closer the way friends grow closer, not the way a mother and daughter should. Her drinking continued to get worse despite her liver disease. This woman who was once strong and determined now seemed intent on drinking herself to death. She didn't want the doctors to know she was drinking heavily because they would not try treatments on her or keep her on the liver transplant list if they knew. She would not let anyone else come to her appointments. She would disappear for a couple of days and we would learn that she had been in so much pain she went to a hospital; she wouldn't tell us so we wouldn't be able to tell the doctors about her drinking.

That Christmas, I went back to Maryland for a visit and met a boy that I kept in contact with. We talked all the time and I eventually decided to move back for him. I ended my California dream in 1998 and moved back for a guy who was a drug dealer, which got me heavier into drugs. I lived with my dad even though he still treated me the way he had when I was a teenager. After a couple of years, my mom got so sick that she came back too. My dad let her take over the master suite and he slept in another bedroom. I was her primary caretaker as she continued to get worse and worse. My dad would take care of her some at night, but I remember him waking me up and saying, "Your turn," and I would get up and clean vomit off of her and get her into bed. I would take care of my mom during the day and do drugs all night to drown out the anger and pain. I was mad at God. I had grown up thinking He was just a God of rules and nothing more. When my mom got sick, I just got angry with Him.

I cut myself for the first time Thanksgiving Day 2001. My mom wasn't there because she was too sick and I didn't enjoy spending the holiday with the rest of the family. I went home and started drinking. I couldn't get in touch with any of my friends. I was just so angry I had to do something; I don't even know where the idea of cutting myself came from. But I did it and it brought a moment of relief. There was a rush like adrenaline from working up to do it, a rush from the act of cutting and the pain and the blood, and then a rush from cleaning it up. It was like a quick high. It was something I felt like I had control over when I didn't have control over anything else in my life. The cutting isolated me: I wanted to cut again because I felt isolated and the cycle continued just like it did with the drugs that brought momentary relief.

My mom seemed to be trying to kill herself with alcohol in the face of her liver disease. By the time she really knew it would kill her, it was too late. She was so proud she didn't want anybody to know what was going on with her and how bad it really was, but eventually there was no avoiding it. She had a couple of falls and ended up in a rehab facility for two months. We soon realized that she was malnourished because nobody was making sure she ate; they just left a tray of food and later someone came back and took away the tray that was still full of food and nobody did anything. She ended up with problems from not eating and problems from bedsores.

Eventually the alcohol and her disease did kill her. From the rehab facility she went to the hospital; they took her off the transplant list because she would have been too weak to survive the surgery. They sent her home, and, after three weeks of hospice care, she was gone. All of this only added to my anger with God. I was so mad and so hurt but I tried not to show any emotion; I just drowned it out with drugs and self-harm. After she died, my dad caught me stealing a bunch of money and kicked me out. I hated my dad but he had only treated me the same way he had been treated by his parents. I had been falling into this pit for years, but now I was at rock bottom.

I was looking for a place to stay and ended up with a friend's mom. The mom had conditions for letting me live there: no drugs were allowed, of course, and I had to go to church with her. I was finally ready for help and I accepted those conditions. I had grown up in a mainline Protestant church, but we stopped going when I was a teenager. I only knew about the God of rules; I didn't know anything about a relationship with God. I went to church with my friend's mom and there I saw people freely praising God and showing love. With the atmosphere there, I cried and cried through every service because I just couldn't contain it anymore. I finally felt like there was some hope for my life again. The Holy Spirit drew me in and I finally started a real relationship with Jesus Christ.

The church let me work there and save money until I found a place to go. The church secretary was helping me look for programs, but what we were finding were secular programs that were 30-90 days. She eventually found Teen Challenge, but it was a year-long program. I didn't want to go away for a year! With a little more time going to that church and my small group there, I realized that a strict year-long program was exactly what I needed, so I packed my bags for Teen Challenge in Philadelphia.

Teen Challenge is a very structured recovery program. We had sixteen girls in the house; our days were filled with prayer time, classes, and chores. Every night, we had an activity like going to a local church or a Bible study group. We were not allowed to listen to the radio or watch television, except for news and Bible studies. CDs had to be approved and we were only allowed to listen to praise music. It was strict, but strict is what some of us need to recover. When I started going to church services in Teen Challenge, I still cried my way through them. Over time, things got better, and I finally started to grow and truly feel love in my relationship with Him. Jesus used Teen Challenge to save my life.

I really thrived with the structure at Teen Challenge. Growing up, my parents didn't care what I did as long as I wasn't bothering them. In the program, we got money from churches that would take a love offering after we came and did praise music or danced and gave our testimonies. At first, I didn't talk about my cutting in my testimony. At one church, we were doing praise and a guy saw my scars. He talked to me after the service and told me not to be ashamed of my scars, that they were part of my testimony. After that, I started sharing my experiences with cutting. Every time I shared, people would come and thank me for talking about it. Every time I spoke, I would meet someone who was a cutter themselves or knew somebody that was. Parents would come and talk to me about their kids and young people would talk to me about their friends. Years later, I've had a counselor and a pastor call me for help working with a cutter.

Teen Challenge was harder than I thought, not because of escaping from substance abuse, but because I had to start feeling again and work through the hurts in my life. I finally had to mourn for my mom. While I was in the program, my dad started coming to see me. He hugged me for the first time and said "I love you" for the first time in my life. I started dealing with my hatred for him. I realized that hurt people hurt other people and that he had been raised much worse than we had. I realized that my mom had talked bad about him all the time. I realized he worked all the time at two different jobs because my mom's spending was as out of control as her drinking. I also had to work with continuing anger toward my mom about her not trying to fight her liver disease; she would probably still be alive today if she had made better choices with her health.

After my year in the program, I came home and eventually got a job at a doctor's office. By God's grace, I worked my way up from receptionist to personal secretary to office manager. While I had been in Teen Challenge, I had met a woman who volunteered there and we stayed in contact after I graduated. We went to a Joyce Meyer[1] conference together and I started pouring my heart out about the man of my dreams and what he would be like. "Sounds like my son," was her reply. I had cried out to God that I couldn't meet someone by myself and He heard me. She gave me her son's number; we started talking and eventually met at church. He had been through Teen Challenge too. Barry and I got married on Mother's Day weekend a year later.

Right after we were married, I became pregnant, but I miscarried our first baby. I became pregnant again right away, but they told me she had fluid on her brain and might not live; if she did, she might be severely disabled. The doctors could run some tests, but they told me those could lead to miscarriage. I found myself at the same hospital I was born in with doctors going over termination options and trying to convince me to have an abortion, just like they did with my mom. They showed me a binder of pictures of disabled children to try and convince me to have an abortion. Like my mom, I wouldn't even consider killing my child.

Abigail was born with significant issues like autism and epilepsy, but she didn't even have the problems they had diagnosed her with in the womb. When she was born, they took her to the NICU, but eventually brought her back and said she was fine. We could tell she had a breathing problem. A couple of days after she was born, a doctor came in who immediately realized what was wrong: she had flaps of skin blocking her nasal airways. They took her to a children's hospital that was able to do the surgery she needed. Over the first year, she had to have surgery four times because the scar tissue would end up sealing off her airway again. Eventually this problem was solved, but we continue to work through treatments for autism and epilepsy. Abigail can be a challenge, but she brings so much joy to us. She still doesn't speak, but she has a communication device that lets us interact with her.

After Abigail was born, we moved from Maryland to Alabama for Barry's new job. I got involved in a good Celebrate Recovery group there that really helped me. I had two more miscarriages before our second daughter, Emma, was born. She was born healthy and without the same challenges her sister has had. She has been such an amazing help and blessing. I went through times of hopelessness and exhaustion and burnout, but my church and my Celebrate Recovery group helped. Eventually, we moved back to New Jersey, where Barry is from, so his mom could help us and because laws there required that our health insurance pay for Abigail's therapy.

When we moved back to New Jersey, I had the girls mostly on my own for the first few weeks and I found myself so angry I couldn't contain it. I was so emotional and was lashing out at everyone. It turned out I was pregnant again. I got so excited about this pregnancy. I felt a new sense of hope, like I had a chance to really get it right this time after what I felt were so many mistakes before. That sense of hope and excitement was what made my final miscarriage so devastating.

I began to have some relapses with both drugs and cutting as I was trying to cope. I almost went back to Teen Challenge. I sometimes get jealous of Barry because he stopped drugs immediately when he got saved, while, for me, it is like the thorn in the side that the Apostle Paul described[2]. After my relapses, my anger toward my mom grew; she could still be here if she had stopped drinking and taken care of herself. And the more I fight addiction for the

SCARS ON HER HEART – LAUREN'S STORY

sake of my children, the more anger I have over my mom giving up and not fighting for our sake. When the hospice care first started, the nurse asked a ton of questions, including my mother's religious beliefs. Mom said she felt like God had forsaken her and burst into tears. When I got into Teen Challenge, I started wondering where my mom went when she died. After telling my counselor about how my mom felt forsaken, she said that it sounds like Mom was a believer and could be in heaven. My aunt later told me that she had led Mom through the sinner's prayer[3] before she passed away. I still struggle with anger towards her, but so many of my memories of her were good. I loved her very much.

Barry and I started having more marriage problems during this time too and even talked about separation. I talked to my pastor and a counselor, who offered to work with me for free. This counselor and a great Celebrate Recovery sponsor have helped me recover and stay clean for good. They have helped me handle memories of my mom and the times she drank with us. God's grace and the godly counselors[4] in my life have helped me make it through.

There were so many times in my life that God's grace kept me in this world even though I was trying my best to leave it. I wrecked so many cars while I was driving drunk or high. I did so many different types of drugs at once I started having seizures; I even had a seizure while driving and wrecked once. God had His hand on me all the time. Jesus had a purpose for my life and never listened to my pleas to leave this world.

Now I have been sober for the longest I've ever been and Jesus is there beside me with every step I take. In some ways, it's easier in Teen Challenge, where all you have to do is study and pray. Now, even when I start to feel myself falling away and failing when I try in my own strength, I know the Lord is with me and in relationship with me and it is through His strength that I can do all things[5].

Abigail has become a great worshipper; it's really the only time she sits still. She laughs and smiles and lifts her hands and worships God. She has sat through a 90-minute praise service just worshipping Him! Emma loves the Lord and I don't know what I would do without her. She helps with everything and takes care of Abigail, showing her such compassion. It's hard for her when so much attention has to go to Abigail, but she handles it so well.

My dad had a stroke a couple of years ago and started to slip into dementia, slowly losing his cognitive ability. Before his mental decline began, Barry was there helping him with something and started talking about the Lord. Dad started crying and saying, "Why would God forgive me?" He knew about God but he never really knew God until that day. My husband led my father to Christ! Now I know where Dad will be when he leaves this earth.

Jesus' love, acceptance, and protection have become better than any high. Even after my failures and hard times, He always pulls me back in. The change in my life when Jesus came into it is the only reason I'm still here. There is no way I could have done anything without God or without the great support system He provided through church, my Christian counselor, and my Celebrate Recovery sponsor. Now Barry and I are persevering in prayer for our other family members who have not yet accepted the love of Jesus Christ.

More to Think About from Lauren

Like her husband Barry, Lauren won her first battles over substance abuse at a Teen Challenge center. But for her, substance abuse continued to be a thorn in her side long after she graduated from the Teen Challenge program. She received continued help from a Christian counselor and from a program called Celebrate Recovery. Celebrate Recovery started at Rick Warren's Saddleback Church and has grown into an international ministry that helps people overcome many issues in their lives, including substance abuse. There is a Celebrate Recovery program in practically every city and town in America. For Lauren, her Celebrate Recovery sponsor was integral to being free from substance abuse once and for all.

Lauren also struggled with feelings of anger toward God. She experienced a very common tendency to blame God for the evil in the world and the bad things that happen. The reality is that we live in a fallen world, one full of broken people, with a real enemy who seeks to steal, kill, and destroy[6]. Even in this broken world full of sin, God can use the pain and evil of the world for His purposes and turn it for good. C.S. Lewis once said that pain is God's megaphone. In Lewis' book *Problem of Pain*[7], he explains the reality of pain and evil in the world. God does not set out to do us harm and bring us pain, but He is able to use even those things for good if we let Him.

Like Ashleigh Grace, Lauren had another great struggle in her life: self-harm. Cutting provided a kind of relief that Lauren felt she had control over. In actuality, it was part of a swirl of depression and addictions that were very difficult to overcome. Lauren was ultimately able to overcome this as well through the power of the Holy Spirit and the help of counselors and sponsors. There are now a number of resources to help with self-harm, including To

Write Love On Her Arms[8], which grew from a simple online plea to an international nonprofit that has become the subject of a feature film. If you are struggling with self-harm, eating disorders, or mental health issues, you are not alone. There are people waiting to help you without judgment; most of all the love of Christ Jesus is there for you. Finally, if you or someone you know is currently considering suicide, call the suicide hotline[9] any time at 1-800-273-8255. Reach out to a pastor or a Christian counselor to help you see that Jesus loves you and has more in store for your life on this earth.

Prayer verse

Jeremiah 29:11 (NIV) "For I know the plans I have for you," declares the Lord, "plans to prosper you and not to harm you, plans to give you hope and a future."

Lord Jesus, I know evil comes not from You, but from sin in this fallen world full of people who deny You in word or action. I believe that your grace is sufficient to help me overcome every thorn in my side and every problem that seems so impossible to me. You are not done with me …

63 Years – Ken's Story

In the fall of 2006, at the age of 68, I was volunteering with Kairos Prison Ministry for the first time. We were doing a weekend program inside Limestone Correctional Facility in North Alabama, and, that Saturday night, along with a group of 42 inmates, I was listening to the final talk in a series about forgiveness. The speaker told all of us, team members and inmates, to take out a clean sheet of paper and write down the names of anyone we needed to forgive. I thought and thought, but I couldn't for the life of me call to mind someone I needed to forgive. At the end of the talk, we are told to pray for the Holy Spirit to bring to mind the name of anyone for whom we harbor ill will or hold in unforgiveness. As soon as I started that prayer, the Holy Spirit spoke in a still, small voice and said, "What about Henry?" I was stunned! I heard it again, and, in this time of reverent prayer, I replied to the Lord and said, "You don't mean that bastard that murdered my mother, do you?"

My great-great-grandparents on my father's side emigrated from Germany to eastern Pennsylvania about 1850. Shortly thereafter, they crossed the Delaware River to the Garden State, New Jersey. To my knowledge, the next three generations of children were all truck farmers, raising fruit and vegetables on small farms as opposed to raising grain, cotton, soybeans, etc., on large farms. Truck farming at that time was heavy manual labor, six days a week, from sunrise to sunset. It was into this environment that I was born in Mt. Holly, New Jersey, just a few miles from the family farms, in 1938.

Although I have a very limited memory of my early life on our farm, there are a few things I do recall. At the age of five, I remember my mother giving me a bath in a washtub in our kitchen; at that time, we did not have an indoor bathroom. I'm sure that I received more than one bath in five plus years, but I only remember one. Related to not having an indoor bathroom, I do have one vivid, not-so-pleasant memory: our outhouse!

Although I was born during the Great Depression, our family was always blessed with having sufficient food to eat, primarily because my mother, grandmother, and aunt canned fruit and vegetables all summer. My dad loved homemade ice cream. Except for a small Allis Chalmers tractor and the farm truck, the only other gas-powered gadget on the farm was an ice cream churn. It was a homemade device that in no way would meet today's OSHA standards, but it cranked out some good ice cream.

Henry was a hired hand that worked around the farm. Even though he had been disabled by polio as a child, he got around quite well on crutches. Henry was a jack-of-all-trades when it came to repairing farm equipment, so my dad hired him on a part-time basis to do just that, keep the farm equipment running.

The one thing I remember about Henry is that he gave me a hatchet for my sixth birthday. For a six-year-old, it was the best of all possible gifts. My hatchet had a smooth wooden handle, a shiny sharp blade, and a leather blade protector. I tested my hatchet on some small saplings that had grown up around the barn. I placed my hatchet under my bed for safekeeping, but not for long. The next day Henry dulled my hatchet, supposedly for my safety, on one of the large rocks that lined our driveway. My hatchet had large chips in the blade. It was useless! I cried and took it to the outhouse and bid it goodbye.

I hated Henry!

Just two months after my sixth birthday, on a pleasant July evening in 1944, Dad was tending his corn crop in the field across the road from our home. I was playing in the front yard while Mother and my two younger sisters were inside. Mother hurriedly gathered her children together and was headed down the driveway toward the road with my younger sisters, Fay and Ruth, in a baby carriage and me in tow. From sensing the anxiety in my mother's voice, I realized that something was terribly wrong. Before we were halfway down the driveway, a shot rang out and I saw my mother collapse, struck by a single shot to the temple from a small caliber pistol.

I raced across the yard, jumped the ditch, crossed the road, and headed through the cornfield to find my dad. Together, we returned to the front yard and we saw the tragedy: Mother laying on the gravel driveway in a pool of blood, my two sisters still in the baby carriage and Henry lying on the front porch.

Not knowing why Henry was in this position, Dad approached cautiously and found that Henry had turned the gun on himself. He appeared to be alive, but unconscious. The pistol was on the front porch floor next to Henry. Dad picked up the pistol and pointed it at Henry, ready to empty the remaining four shots into Henry's head when he heard a still, small voice say, "Don't do it." Hearing that voice, Dad tossed the gun a safe distance away and went to see what he could do for his wife and daughters.

By that time, a neighbor had called the sheriff, and, within a few minutes, both the sheriff and an ambulance arrived. Mother and Henry were placed in the same ambulance. The neighbors took care of my sisters and me. Dad followed the ambulance to the hospital. Mother died in the ambulance. Henry survived his self-inflicted gunshot through his mouth and neck.

At the age of six, I was not ready to be a motherless child.

Who was going to tuck me in at night?

Who would fix my breakfast?

Who would hold me when I was afraid?

Who would take me to my first day of school that fall?

Sometimes God knows that we need Him and He sends people to be His voice, His hands and feet, His hugs and kisses, His tears, His compassion.

Many people came to the aid of our grieving family, including neighbors, family members, law enforcement, a compassionate judge, and people we did not even know.

At Mother's visitation a couple of days after her death, Dad helped me place three white roses in her hands, representing her three children. That's my last memory of my mother.

The untimely death of my mother had a major emotional effect on my life.

I jumped at the sound of loud noises.

I had nightmares.

I became a bed-wetter.

I couldn't get out of my mind the picture of my mother in her casket, holding the roses from her three children.

Mother's death also impacted my dad to the point that he sold the farm and recommitted his life to Christ. Knowing that he could not raise three children by himself, my three-year old sister went to live with dad's sister and my one-year old sister went to live with Mother's sister. Dad and I moved into my paternal grandparents' home.

As the only witness to my mother's murder, the judge who had been assigned the case asked Dad to bring me to the courthouse to speak with him. I recall going up the courthouse stairs and Dad telling me to not be afraid and to just tell the judge what I saw. We were accompanied to the courtroom and the judge came down from the bench and asked us to sit down on one of the benches at the side of the room. He pulled up a chair and I told him everything I had seen. At the end of the meeting, Dad told the judge that he and the family did not want Henry to be given a death sentence. We learned that Henry had pleaded guilty and was sentenced to life in the New Jersey State Prison in Trenton. Near the end of his life, Dad shared what he believed the motive was: he had heard that Henry was in love with my mother and that he wasn't willing to let anyone else have her if he couldn't.

I still hated Henry.

My paternal grandparents, especially my grandmother, were very loving. She did everything possible to cheer and encourage me. She loved to tell Bible stories. I still remember some of her stories like "Jonah and the Whale[1]," "Daniel in the Lion's Den[2]," and "Jesus in the Manger[3]." Grandma didn't just read the stories from the King James Bible; she filled in the details, not just with words, but with animation. I can see her now describing the whale by spreading out her arms and clamping down on me. It scared me, but she was quick to turn that big bite into a big hug and kiss. She loved to take the train to shop in Philadelphia and we had great times going to the city.

Grandpa was a man of few words. He was up at daybreak and, following breakfast, he was headed to the field or orchard until exactly noon. If you were in the field with him, you would see him checking his Hamilton pocket watch when it was getting near noon. He was never late for lunch: at 11:55, he was at the water pump at the back of the house, washing his hands and face. His pocket watch is a keepsake that I treasure today.

Grandpa and my Uncle Wilmer were expert farmers. Grandpa's specialty was cantaloupes and sweet corn and my uncle's was peaches and strawberries. Any time I was in the field or barns with Grandpa, he would be showing me how to do whatever task was at hand. It was at this early stage of farming that I figured out that this would definitely not be my career.

Dad and I stayed with my grandparents for a year or so after Mother's death. While living there, Dad worked at multiple jobs like making pipe at a steel mill, helping in the fields and orchards on the two farms, delivering truckloads of produce to the Campbell's Soup Company in Camden, and taking what Campbell's didn't need at the time to the farmer's market in Trenton. Going to the farmer's market was really the only thing that I liked about farming, because Dad would always give me a quarter to buy a hotdog and a bottle of chocolate milk. He'd even tell me to keep the change!

My Uncle Robert, Dad's youngest brother, served as a Marine in World War II. While attacking one of the

Japanese islands, he suffered major shrapnel wounds to both legs. When he was able, they moved him to California to recuperate. After six months or so of rehabilitation, he returned to New Jersey. I remember him coming on crutches into my grandparents' living room with a big smile on his face. I know that this was both a day of joy and pain for the family. Uncle Robert slowly recuperated to the point of playing golf and taking a job as Secretary of the Camden County YMCA. Uncle Robert became one of my primary mentors and encouraged me to attend college. He helped me earn money by providing me with a job at YMCA Camp Ockanickon every summer during my high school and college years.

Perhaps the most memorable event of the year and a half that I lived with my grandparents after Mother's death was a visit to my aunt and uncle's home in Pennsylvania. I was consigned to a couch on the enclosed front porch. I got tucked in under four or five quilts and blankets. I could see the moonlight's glow upon the snow-covered trees across the road. I had not been in bed for more than ten minutes when I heard the faint ringing of bells. At first, I thought that someone had put a record on the Victrola, but the sound of the bells got louder and louder and, soon, I could tell that the bells were coming down the road in front of the house. Coming down the road was a sleigh pulled by two horses. When I recognized the red tasseled hat, I knew it was Santa! I ran into the house and down the stairs, hollering "Uncle Robert, I saw Santa Claus! He just came down the road in a sleigh!" It was several years later that Uncle Robert told me that it was a custom for one of the neighbors to do a Santa sleigh ride on Christmas Eve if the weather permitted. For several years, I had thought they staged the Santa sleigh ride just for a six-and-a-half-year-old motherless boy. It didn't matter. It was the best Christmas ever for me!

In my life, especially those few years after Mother's death, family, friends, and people who I didn't know reached out to help and encourage me when I was hurting. One was the elderly Sunday School teacher at our small church, who taught us and took us to the park and let us swim in the Delaware River. This was an outpouring of God's grace through the heart, voice, hands, and feet of God's people. But I was still frightened by loud noises, I still laid awake at night, and, when I did go to sleep, I had nightmares. I still longed for my mother.

I hated Henry.

December 7, 1945, about seventeen months after Mother's death, was a memorable day for two reasons: it was the fourth anniversary of the Japanese attack on Pearl

Harbor and it was the day that a seven-and-a-half-year-old boy received one of the greatest gifts a motherless child could receive: a new mom and a big sister.

My mother's death had a major impact on my dad. It was shortly thereafter that Dad rededicated his life to Jesus Christ and was called into the ministry. In the fall of 1945, he enrolled at God's Bible School in Cincinnati, Ohio. It was there that Dad met Irene, who had also been called to ministry. Irene's husband had been killed in an accident at a steel mill in Detroit. Having both experienced the loss of a spouse, they shared each other's life stories and became friends over the period of a few weeks.

To help pay tuition, Dad drove the college bus. One evening, at the end of their second date, which consisted of riding in the college bus to get ice cream at a local drug store, Dad asked, "Irene, do you think you will get married again?" Being somewhat blindsided, Irene responded, "Well, I'm not sure right now." Dad possessed many spiritual gifts, but patience was not one of them. He told Irene, "Well, let me know in the morning!"

That evening, Irene prayed about this proposal and talked about it with her eleven-year-old daughter, Claudia. When Claudia found out that my dad had two young daughters and a son, she was all in since she had had no sisters or brothers. Within a few weeks, Dad and Irene were married. By saying yes, Irene became the mom of four children, three of whom she had not yet met! I called her Mom from day one.

It was Christmas 1945 that my grandmother told me that Dad was coming home from God's Bible School, that he was married, and that I had a new eleven-year-old sister. That was quite a Christmas! Claudia and I were assigned to a bedroom at the top of the stairs. In our pajamas, we just sat in bed and talked, or maybe I should say that Claudia talked, and talked, and talked. I'm not sure what time we went to sleep, if we ever did, but, in those hours, we became good friends, a true brother and sister. Since that time, I have always addressed Claudia as my sister, not my step-sister.

Following the Christmas gathering, Dad and my new mom prepared to move to her home in Dearborn, Michigan. On the way to Dearborn, we stopped to pick up my four-year-old sister in Pennsylvania and then headed on to Dearborn. My youngest sister remained with our aunt and uncle and joined the rest of the family a few months later.

Dad began his ministry as pastor of a small church just west of Detroit, and, after serving there for six months, we moved to a small farm in Romulus, Michigan in the summer of 1946. Dad served as the pastor of Romulus

Wesleyan Methodist Church. With our new family of six and dad's low salary as a minister, he took on extra jobs. He planted and cultivated a large garden, drove a school bus, and did maintenance work at the grammar school as well as odd jobs around town.

A year and a half after moving to Romulus, our family of six grew to seven; I had a brother, Paul. I remember the day Mom and Paul returned home from the hospital. I ran all the way home to see the little fellow. For some reason, I thought I would have a playmate. I had never seen a newborn baby up close; I said, "Look how little he is! I guess it will be some time before we can go ice skating together." Being nine years older than Paul, we never had the opportunity to really "play" with each other.

In 1948, our family came close to having another tragic event. Paul, at fifteen or sixteen months old, while playing outside, fell head first into a ten-gallon crock that was used to catch rainwater from one of the downspouts at home. Had it not been for a telephone repairman that happened to be close by and had been trained in artificial respiration, Paul would not have survived.

When I think back to the few years following the death of my mother, I realize that even through tragedies "that all things (do) work together for good[4]." After being a motherless child, God had placed a big sister and a wonderful mom in my life, a lady that was in every respect a mother to me. Over that period of three years, I became less afraid of the dark, loud noises did not bother me, and I ceased to have nightmares.

But I still hated Henry.

After living in Romulus for three years, we moved to Central, a small town of 500 people, in western South Carolina. There were two reasons we moved: Dad wanted to continue his ministerial education and he wanted a change of climate. A couple feet of snow on the ground from Thanksgiving to Easter in Michigan was a bit too much.

Our family of seven moved into a two-bedroom/one-bathroom house, which was a little tight, to say the least. We lived just off campus near Central Wesleyan College (now Southern Wesleyan University). Dad took on the pastorate of two churches: Pickens View and Martin Grove, both Wesleyan Methodist churches.

I do not recall the date that I accepted Christ as my Savior, but it was at age twelve that I walked down the aisle and knelt at the altar on a Sunday evening at the Central Wesleyan Methodist Church on the college campus. I can't say that I had a profound change of heart, mind, or character, but I knew one thing: I was a child of God[5].

Dad's pastoral income from the two small churches was not sufficient to support a family of seven, so he took on various side jobs: produce manager at the local grocery store, second shift worker at a cotton mill, clerk at a men's store, a house-to-house dry cleaning delivery route, and printing press operator. And, though our yard was small, he planted a vegetable garden behind the house.

As if pastoring two churches and working part-time jobs was not enough to keep Dad busy, he started a Boy Scout troop of six or seven boys in the neighborhood. I came to love the outdoors, camping, bicycling, and canoeing, but not so much hiking. It was my opinion that if you could bike or canoe, why hike? Scouting was a positive venture for me that helped to bring me out of my depression over the loss of my mother.

Living less than a quarter mile from the high school, on the first day of my freshman year, two or three of my friends and I placed ourselves in a perfect viewing position in the administration building, less than 50 yards from the girls' dormitory. Wow! I knew right away that high school was going to be great; I had never seen so many beautiful young ladies. Over the next year or so, my fondness of the

Boy Scouts waned and my interest in the fairer sex increased.

During the summer months following my freshman year, I worked as a counselor at a YMCA camp. Being 500 miles from most of these young ladies, I thought it would be a good idea to keep in contact with them. I wrote each of them a letter. Each of them responded to my letter and we corresponded throughout the summer. Little did I know that, a few years later, I would marry one of these young ladies.

About the middle of our sophomore year in high school, Jane and I started to hang out together after class and in the evenings. Being less than sixteen, the minimum age for dating at the school, we just had to steal away whenever and wherever possible in order to be together. Our relationship was not entirely consistent -- we had a couple of break-ups -- but, thanks to my persistence, it didn't take more than a few weeks to get back together.

I loved the environment of our high school and junior college. The rules and regulations of the school were strict, but, in looking back, I know that it was good for me. For the most part, it kept me out of trouble and strengthened my faith in Christ. In September 1957, I enrolled as a junior at Guilford College, just outside of Greensboro, North Carolina. About the same time, at the

TESTIMONIES OF GRACE

age of nineteen, with about $100 in my pocket and two more years of college ahead, it was with fear and trepidation that I asked Jane's dad for her hand in marriage. I had expected him to say, "Well, Ken, why don't you come back in a couple years when you can support my daughter." I was bowled over when he said, "Yes," and gave me her hand. Up until that time, this was my happiest day ever!

But I still hated Henry!

Jane and I were married on September 7, 1958, just a few days before my senior year in college. At this point, I had about $300 in my pocket, but, with the help of wedding gifts, my job maintaining the landscaping at the church and adjoining cemetery, and Jane's full-time job at Southern Bell, we were able to pay tuition and to rent a small trailer about five miles off campus, right across the street from the church I had attended for my junior year in college and next door to its parsonage. The rent was $35 per month, including water and electricity. In addition to our low rent and utilities, the pastor and his lovely wife would have us over for dinner once or twice per week.

Following graduation in May 1959, with a degree in mathematics, I worked for three years at Pilot Life Insurance Company in the claims and actuarial department.

133

It didn't take long for our family of two to expand to four: our son, Robert, born November 7, 1959, and our daughter, Linda, on July 3, 1961.

By the summer of 1962, I realized that the insurance business was not for me. Having seen an advertisement in the *Atlanta Journal* for programmers at Brown Engineering in Huntsville, Alabama, I sent my resume and a cover letter to the company, and, without the first inkling of what programming was, they hired me, put me through a two-week training session, and sent five other young men and me out to Marshall Space Flight Center in Huntsville.

Computers were in their infancy in 1962. There were no college degrees in Computer Science at that time and the art of software development was in pre-infancy. Our team of six worked ten- to twelve-hour days learning and doing by trial and error until we mastered the job. This job was the beginning of my career as a program analyst. Over the course of 49 years in software development, I never had a job that I did not like. I could not have asked for a better career. Life was good.

But I still hated Henry!

One Sunday morning in 2005, my friend, Sidney, said, "Hey, Ken, I know I've invited you to attend a Walk to Emmaus[6] several times in the past two or three years, but I just thought that this might be the right time for you."

The Walk to Emmaus begins with an invitation from a sponsor. It is an experience of Christian spiritual renewal that begins with a three-day course in Christianity. These three days provide the attendees, referred to as pilgrims, an opportunity to meet Jesus Christ in a new way as God's grace and love is revealed to them through other believers.

It was in March 2006, that Sidney came by the house and we headed off to Camp Sumatanga in Gallant, Alabama, about 100 miles from home and about fifteen miles from civilization and cell phone service. The first thing I noticed in the auditorium at the camp was three tables full of food. I thought, "I think I'm going to be okay here at Sumatanga." This feeling didn't last too long. After introductions all around and a short devotional, the leader said, "Okay, guys, we are going to all head to the dorm, but here's what I want you to do: as you go to the dorm, please be silent and maintain that silence until we let you know sometime tomorrow."

Well, the silence didn't last long in my room. Within a few minutes after going to bed, my two roommates started a duet: One snored tenor and the other snored bass. I wrapped my head in my pillow, covered my ears as much as possible, and just laid there until what seemed like almost daybreak when I finally dozed off. Just about the time I had fallen asleep, I was startled by the ringing of cowbells and some sub-humans singing off-tune in the hallway, "Rise and Shine and Give God the Glory, Glory..." I made it through the Benedictine silence, the duet, the ringing of cowbells, and the off-tune singing. Just before breakfast, the silence was lifted and we began day one of my Walk to Emmaus. These three days were life-changing for me.

Following the three-day experience, participants are joined in small groups to support each other in their ongoing walk with Christ. Through the formational process of accountable discipleship in small groups and participation in the Emmaus community, each participant's individual gifts and servant-leadership skills are developed for use in the local church and its mission. Participants are encouraged to find ways to live out their individual call to discipleship. Prior to my Walk to Emmaus, I had lived a sheltered life. My Christian life had been one of church administration, serving as church treasurer, leading fundraisers for new church facilities, serving on multiple building committees, serving as chair of the Administration Board, etc. After my Walk, my Christian-life priority pivoted from administration to mission.

I always hate it when someone says, "God told me to tell you…" as if God had to have a middleman to call me up. On the way home from Camp Sumatanga, Sidney, my Walk to Emmaus sponsor, didn't use those words. He was more direct.

He said, "Hey Ken, you're going to serve on Kairos 43. It is coming up in a few months."

I said, "I am? What is Kairos?"

"Oh, it's Emmaus behind bars. Don't worry; we'll be going to some training sessions that will bring you up to speed before we go in."

By this time, I had gotten used to Sidney telling me what God wanted me to do, so I agreed. The mission of Kairos Prison Ministry is to share the transforming love and forgiveness of Jesus Christ and to impact the hearts and lives of incarcerated men, women, and youth, as well as their families, so that they may become loving and productive citizens of their communities.

My assigned position at the weekend program for Kairos 43 was to be a Family Servant; in other words, I was to make sure the six inmates and three team members at my table had coffee, lemonade, cookies, lunch, and dinner. All the gray-heads on the Kairos team told me how great it was to be a family servant: "The best position I've ever had!"

they said. What they didn't know was that I had experienced essential tremor since about the age of 50.

Essential tremor is a neurological disorder that causes an involuntary and rhythmic tremor. It can affect almost any part of your body, but the trembling occurs most often in your hands, especially when you do intentional tasks, such as using a fork or knife to cut a steak, buttoning shirts, tying shoelaces, or simply carrying a cup of coffee.

At our last team meeting prior to our Kairos weekend, I told our lead family servant that I was getting a little antsy about pouring coffee, tea, and lemonade at prison. I could just see myself splashing a cup of hot coffee all over a tough inmate. He listened as I described my tremor and I gave him a demonstration involving trying to carry two cups full of water; it wasn't pretty!

This didn't seem to trouble him. He simply said, "Lets pray about it." He gathered up the other six table servers, who all surrounded me, placing their hands on my shoulders and praying. They prayed that God would simply control my hands during the weekend. I served the nine men at my table all weekend without spilling a drop of coffee or anything else. My hands were rock-steady throughout the weekend. This simple miracle gave me the assurance that God is there for us; all we have to do is ask.

I wish that the prayer hadn't been limited to four days because come Monday morning, my tremor was back to normal.

One of the main themes of a Kairos weekend is forgiveness, and, by Saturday night, we were listening to the final talk before holding a forgiveness ceremony in which we would offer up names of those we needed to forgive. Then I got out my paper, prayed for the Holy Spirit to bring any names to mind, and heard him ask about Henry.

I wrote Henry's full name on my sheet of paper and shortly afterward we all went outside, formed a circle, and, table-by-table, we prayed, asking God to accept our acts of forgiveness. We placed our lists in a metal bucket. When all of the lists were in the bucket, one of the clergy members set fire to the lists. As I watched the smoke ascend into the night sky, I felt a burden lifted off my shoulders that I had carried for 63 years.

I forgave Henry.

A few months after my first Kairos weekend, I began to live out my new focus on mission, my ministry now two-fold: coordinating a monthly worship service at Limestone Correctional Facility and helping inmates who are paroled or who have reached the end of their sentence.

In the past twelve years, I have helped a dozen or more ex-inmates by providing transportation home on the day they were released, helping them locate a halfway house, paying their rent at a halfway house or motel, and providing clothing, furniture, food, hygiene products, and more.

At the end of 2015, I felt compelled to broaden my prison ministry. In a conversation with the chaplain at the Limestone Correctional Facility, I asked him if I could serve as an assistant chaplain at Limestone. He said yes. I went through the necessary training, and since then I have served as an assistant chaplain one day per week.

What I have learned from my experience as an assistant chaplain is that not all inmates are villains. For many of the inmates in prison, the very act of incarceration is a turning point in their lives, turning away from sin and riotous living toward a Christ-centered life. I know that we have all heard the term "jailhouse religion," and, while it is a fact in some cases, for many, it is not. Having talked one-on-one to hundreds of men in the course of my ministry, dozens have told me that being incarcerated is the best thing that happened to them. I always ask, "Why?" and their response is, "If I hadn't been incarcerated, I wouldn't be alive today. If drugs didn't kill me, I would have been killed or seriously wounded in a gang fight." In addition, many of them have said that they probably would not have accepted

Jesus Christ as their savior outside of prison, primarily because they had strayed away from Christ and the church in their teens. Prison is a dark place. Were it not for the light of Christ that is manifested by many of the inmates, it would be even darker. Some of the most dedicated Christians that I have ever known are in prison, or, as ex-felons, are now living a Christ-centered life on the outside.

I've asked myself several times, "Why prison? Are there not easier ministries?" After more than a decade in prison ministry, I've come to the conclusion that it all had to do with Henry, the man who murdered my mother. Many times I thought about Henry and his incarceration in the New Jersey state prison in Trenton. I can only hope that there was a chaplain, a religious volunteer, or an inmate that led him to Christ, even if he was on his deathbed; it's never too late to accept God's grace or forgiveness[7].

Dad and I seldom talked about the murder of my mother or about Henry. Once, while visiting him when he was 101 years old, I asked him when he forgave Henry. His answer was, "When I threw the gun aside." I thought, "Wow! It took Dad a few minutes to forgive Henry, it took me 63 years." But it doesn't matter whether it is a few minutes or 63 years, it is never too early or too late to forgive someone who has done you wrong.

From the time Dad was 99 years old, his family would celebrate his birthday with him each year. When he was 102, he needed to have his pacemaker replaced; he told the surgeon he wanted one with longer battery life this time and the surgeon laughed and offered him a lifetime warranty. His 103rd and 104th celebrations were at the nursing home where he lived. The nursing home staff sponsored his 104th birthday party for him and invited his family members and nursing home neighbors to join in the celebration. Dad was in good spirits and had a good time playing bingo and eating birthday cake.

According to his roommate, at 6:15 am, just two weeks after his 104th birthday, dad woke up, sat up in bed, and said, "Well, praise the Lord. I'm going Home. I'm going to be with Jesus. I'm going to be with Irene." When the nurse checked on him at 6:30, dad had relocated from the nursing home to his heavenly Home. I hope that when my time comes, I will be like Dad and say, "Well, praise the Lord. I'm going Home."

More to Think About from Ken

Ken's story is a powerful example of the necessity of forgiveness. Like accepting God's grace for salvation, it is never too late to forgive. Ken waited 63 years to forgive; after he did, he decided to find out what happened to Henry and learned that Henry had died in prison almost 50 years earlier. Ken had hated a dead man for nearly half a century! There is an old saying about unforgiveness being a poison that you drink hoping it will harm the other person. Of course, in reality, it only harms you. This is why Jesus put such an emphasis on forgiveness, even putting it in the Lord's Prayer: Forgive others as you have been forgiven[8]. We will never completely walk in the freedom of Christ until we learn to forgive.

The scriptures are full of verses on the importance of forgiveness, as noted even in the words of Jesus Himself. There are also innumerable resources on the topic of forgiveness. Ken's favorite is a pamphlet called *The Forgiveness of God*, written by Mart DeHaan[9], as part of the Discovery Series from Our Daily Bread Ministries. In it, DeHaan starts with our need to forgive ourselves and accept God's total forgiveness of us through Christ's finished work of the cross. He goes on to cover the aspects of God's forgiveness before covering the forgiveness of people. It is important to realize that forgiveness does not mean putting yourself in a position to be hurt again. Forgiving an embezzler doesn't mean you put them in charge of the treasury; forgiving an abuser doesn't mean you let them work in the nursery; and forgiving someone who has harmed you doesn't mean you allow them to remain in your life if they are unsafe. Forgiveness for some is quick, like it was for Ken's father; for others, it is a process that requires going to God for His grace again and again. Ways you will know you have forgiven include your emotions when you think of the person or event, whether you maintain any ill will or desire to get even, and whether you continue to tell people the story in a gossiping sense to make sure as many people know as possible. If you have a surge of anger when you hear a name, want to get back at them some way, or talk about it over and over for no beneficial reason, it may be time to go back to God in prayer for that hurt.

Other books on the topic of forgiveness include *Total Forgiveness* by R.T. Kendall[10], *Helping People Forgive* by David W. Augsburger[11], and *Five Steps to Forgiveness* by Everett Worthington[12]. These all give real scripture-based and practical advice on how to forgive those who have wronged you and to forgive yourself. Whether you use these resources or stick with the scriptures and prayer, forgiveness is a fundamental element of the Christian life. No matter what trauma we have experienced, we are called to forgive.

Prayer verse

Matthew 6:14-15 (NIV) For if you forgive other people when they sin against you, your heavenly Father will also forgive you. But if you do not forgive others their sins, your Father will not forgive your sins.

Lord Jesus, I know that You have called me to forgive and that I can't live a healthy, whole life without forgiving those who have harmed me. Call to my mind right now those who I continue to hold in unforgiveness and grant me your grace to forgive them …

Driving Backwards – Sadie's Story

"I see you are feeling alone, helpless, and unwanted. When have you felt that way before?" My counselor asked that same question for years. I would come to her with a triggering event; someone or something in my life would elicit pain in my heart and, after pressing into that current pain, she would ask me to go back to the first time I remembered feeling the same way[1]. We would do the hard work of sifting through memories until we would come to the earliest memory possible and then we would hit a wall. Something kept me from the breakthrough she was trying to lead me through. My Licensed Professional Counselor knew if she could get me to go backward to face the pain of the original wound of being abandoned by my father that I then could find healing from my Heavenly Father.

"How did you feel when this colleague propositioned you?"

"I can't believe I would be tempted like this! I adore my husband! I am humiliated to admit that, when my professional colleague started telling me how desirable I was and propositioned me for an affair, it turned my head. I was tempted. His words got in my head and it was hard to turn away from. I lingered in his presence for far too long, but, with strength from meditating on Proverbs 7[2] I refused an affair."

"So why are you coming to me with this, Sadie? You didn't follow through with an affair so, other than confessing and bringing it into the light, what do you think you want from counseling concerning this?"

"I am disappointed with myself. I don't want to feel tempted because of my wounds, yet am drawn to the way his desire for me made me feel. I want to do whatever work needs to be done to make sure that, when temptation comes, I'm strong enough to run away right away. Whatever is making me believe I'm undesirable, I want it to go away."

"I've been seeing you long enough to know how I should process my pain with the Lord, so I would like to use my counseling session today to tell you how I processed this current painful situation."

"Sure, it helps me to know how you have processed pain and we can make adjustments where necessary."

"Well, after I discovered this betrayal of trust, I pressed into the pain to try to summarize how I was feeling;

not what my thoughts were on the subject but what I was feeling. I've learned from you in the past that anytime I start saying, 'I feel like…' I'm dealing with a thought and not an emotion. So I worked with my own heart until I was able to summarize the basic emotions I was feeling: shock, feeling caught off-guard, and not good enough. I felt shocked by someone I trusted at a foundational level, blindsided by the realization that things weren't as I had believed, and overwhelmed with grief over feeling not good enough to remain loyal to."

"That's good, Sadie. You were able to push past the pain from a cognitive level to an emotional level. So what happened next?"

"So I went to prayer. I asked God to help me remember when I felt such shock by someone I trusted before. I remembered my first true love. Even though I always had a 'boyfriend,' someone I hoped would make me feel loved and desirable, from an early age, this was the first time I truly felt romantic love for someone in a deeper way. Anyway, he pressured me sexually in ways I was unfamiliar with, and, though tempted by my desire to be wanted, I didn't take things as far as he wanted. In the height of our relationship, when I believed all was well, he unexpectedly stopped wanting me and instead broke my trust and broke my heart by choosing a much younger girl before ending things with me. I was so shocked that what I thought I had as a long standing solid relationship just vanished unexpectedly. I know it was just a high school relationship, but it hurt so much. While I knew this was similar pain to what I was currently feeling, reviewing it with the Lord in prayer didn't cause the pain to lift so I kept pressing deeper into my memories. I asked God to remind me of any time in my life where I felt this shock before."

"This is good, Sadie. I agree that would be painful to feel rejected by someone you cared about and thought cared for you. But you sensed that wasn't all the Lord was doing? Was there something earlier?"

"I continued asking the Lord if there was something earlier. I was asking Him when the first time was that someone violated my trust in a sexual way and left me feeling shocked and blindsided. Maybe even before I really understood sexual feelings. Suddenly, I was doubled over with grief when the memory hit me. I was about ten when I first met my half-brother. As an only child without her father, I was so excited to have a sibling that I might be able to have a relationship with. We had a good visit together but, while our mothers were in the other room visiting, he started saying he wanted to see me without my clothes on. At that age, I didn't even understand sexual things but knew what was being said was wrong. I was heartbroken and shocked. I felt caught off guard and grieved that a 'brother,' someone I believed I would be able to trust for a pure relationship, had turned out to be untrustworthy and unsafe. I asked him to leave and have never seen him again."

"It sounds like you went backward until you found some of the first violations to your trust that left you feeling shocked, unstable, and unwanted for who you are. This process makes it a bit more understandable why your current situation is so hurtful to you as an adult, doesn't it? What did the Lord say next?"

"Well, as you have taught me, I stayed in the pain, reviewing the emotions of the memory, and then asked the Lord to speak whatever He would want to speak to me concerning it. I asked for truth. I asked for His perspective. I asked if it were true that I wasn't enough."

"And what did He say?"

"The Lord has gotten my attention in a variety of ways in the past. I've been amazed by the things God would place in my path to encourage my heart. It could be scripture, a sermon, a song I hear on the radio, a book or devotional I'm reading, a conversation with a trusted friend, sometimes even in visions in my mind. All evidence of His presence around me, so close, was providing what I needed along my path for me to discover at just the right time. This time, I saw a picture of an eye in my mind. First from the front, then from the side. All of a sudden, scriptures about eyes started filling my heart, all of which were applicable to the current pain as well as to the memories I was processing. First was 2 Chronicles 16:9, "For the eyes of the Lord range throughout the earth to strengthen those whose hearts are fully committed to Him." And then came Zechariah 2:8, "For whoever touches you touches the apple of his eye." I began to weep, the tears streaming down my face. I knew the Lord was telling me that He was right there with me in my pain, that, in every painful circumstance He was with me. He was telling me that as I was seeking after His heart He was strengthening me and that whoever hurts me hurts one of His most precious and valuable possessions. He was showing me that when my brother hurt me, God saw the injustice. When my boyfriend betrayed me, he touched God's treasured child. And now, when I felt betrayed, He was there to strengthen me with this newfound healing. When I began to focus on His goodness, my heart began to heal."

"These are people of God!" I would cry to my counselor over a variety of sessions we had together. "How could they treat me so unjustly?" I spent the next half hour sharing how the decisions of a spiritual mentor had left me feeling unprotected and ended in perceived injustice.

"I felt helpless and unprotected when trying to do what's right," I responded when asked how the situation made me feel.

"And when have you felt helpless and unprotected before?"

I went on to recount times in the workplace when I was aggressively attacked and cornered in my cubicle. "Earlier than that," she would ask. I went back further to times in high school where I was pinned in a corner by a larger student. "Okay, but let's try to press further," she would say. "I remember feeling bullied by someone in elementary school and hoping an older relative at the school would stand up for me and protect me but he didn't." Frustrated, we both knew I still wasn't there yet and our session ended.

I was determined to get to the root of it, so I went back again to try to pick up where we left off. "I guess we should talk about Harold," I said. "I know I felt helpless and unprotected in my years of experiences with him. Harold was my first stepfather. I spent years being used as a pawn in his battle with my mom. His only interest in me was using me to hurt my mom."

"I'm so sorry to hear that as a child you were used in that way, Sadie. I can picture you as a young girl having to deal with things far greater than a young child should and it breaks my heart."

"I suppose this needs a little back story to fully understand my feelings of helplessness and being unprotected. Fearing for my safety after my biological father left, my mother had a brilliant idea that could only be attributed as divine inspiration from the Lord. She proposed that her father, my grandfather, legally adopt me to avoid legally sanctioned, unsupervised visits where my biological father might harm me. In exchange for his consent, he would be released from paying child support and any responsibility of fatherhood. Pleased by this proposal, he took the deal and my grandfather became my legal father.

"The responsibilities of being a single mother weighed heavily on my mom so, when she met Harold not long after my biological father left, she was particularly vulnerable and considered his proposal for marriage a potential benefit to us both. Though she wasn't sure about him, my grandfather gave her some disheartening advice: You have a child who needs a father, so take whoever is willing to take you. Beggars can't be choosers."

"Your mom was told to just take what she could get? That's such a strong message about her value."

"Definitely and it breaks my heart for her. I don't blame her for the decisions she has made. How could she have made any better choices with the influences in her life? And, in all seriousness, how could her parents have advised her any better when considering the influences in their lives!

"Anyway, she married him, and, in her eagerness for me to have a father, she allowed Harold to legally adopt me from my grandfather. In hindsight, this decision turned out to be a serious mistake that she and I would pay for over the next decade. We learned through this experience that decisions made with the motive of trying to meet our own needs rather than decisions based on merit don't end well. She wasn't married to Harold very long. They were married for two years, though they spent the second year separated. Throughout that time Harold never showed much interest in me, or in my mom, for that matter. His lack of loving care for her on the heels of a previously harsh relationship was particularly painful and she sought counselors to help her navigate the situation and improve her marriage. In her quest to improve her marriage, she gleaned knowledge from a variety of counselors, books, and resources. When a colleague named Jack began confiding in her over his own marital trouble, she recommended several of the resources she had discovered. Though he took her recommendations to heart and pursued the resources she proposed, his marriage ultimately dissolved. Over time, Jack was looking to reestablish love and Mom encouraged him to date one of her closest friends, Linda.

"Linda had some medical issues and unexpectedly entered a coma which prematurely ended her life. With Harold's approval, Mom reached out to Jack to be a source of support and comfort for him after losing Linda. Unbeknownst to Mom, Jack began developing feelings for her of his own. Surprised by his affirming words and actions and his admission of interest in her, she confided to Harold that his prolonged lack of effort on their marriage was destructive and that she was concerned that, without his attempts to improve their marriage, she would likely fall in love with another man who expressed loving concern for her.

"Harold reluctantly went to counseling with her yet refused to implement their suggestions or participate in sessions that would require effort on his part. Instead of doing anything to improve the marriage, he threatened Mom: if she left him for someone else, he would take me away from her. She had no idea how far he would go to make that a reality. After seeking counsel and the Lord in prayer, she believed the Lord told her that He would be with her no matter what she chose but that there would be consequences either way. So she chose to end her marriage to Harold and later married her colleague, Jack. Jack was my second and final stepfather and they are still together 30 years later. But Harold made good on his promise."

"So Harold fought for you? Do you think that meant he cared for you?"

"Because he had legally adopted me, the courts awarded him the rights of a father. It didn't matter that he wasn't my real father or that he did not have a relationship with me during the marriage. Courts look at all sorts of factors, such as financial care for a child. Harold fought for every minute he could get -- weekends, two weeks at Christmas, a month over the summer -- and legally his claim was considered valid by the courts because he had adopted me. So this man who was not my father and had only been with my mother for a short time used the court system to take me away from her as much as he could. He used the courts to hurt her in the way that could wound her the most: through her child."

"Sadie, I can see how this injustice left you feeling unprotected and helpless, similar to the way you felt in the workplace, or when cornered or bullied throughout your life. I'm so sorry that you had to experience this pain. Let's go to the Lord in prayer and ask Him if it is true that you are unprotected and helpless."

Many of my counseling sessions focused on feelings of rejection and loneliness and on feeling unwanted, undesirable, and isolated. I lived with these feelings for as long as I could remember. They lived so close to my heart that they seemed a constant companion.

Social media can be a beautiful medium for connection. It can also show you when you've missed out on connection. I sat in the counselor's office explaining how I felt excluded when our friends got together for an outing and we were not included on the invitation.

"I mean, I know it's completely reasonable that people will get together without us at times. I know that others have shared interests and history together that we are not always going to be a part of, but I can't help but be tempted to focus on me and think that our exclusion is because there is something wrong with me."

"You probably feel this more deeply because of pain you've experienced in the past. When have you felt isolated before?"

"I imagine a lot of these feelings of isolation started during my forced visitations with Harold. It was awkward to spend so much time alone with a grown man who wasn't my real father, so I actually spent a lot of that time alone; hiding was preferable to unwanted interaction. On days he had to work, he would wake me up super early to drop me off with one of his many siblings, but most of the time they weren't awake when I would get there so I'd sit alone until they woke up. I begged him to let my mom keep me on those days and he could come back and get me after work. She lived literally across the street from him which would have reduced the travel time and saved me from extra exhaustion and provided me comfort to be with someone I knew loved me deeply. He refused, however, saying it was important to him for me to spend time with his family and not just mine. I can remember countless times on those drives to his family's house seeing my reflection in the window with tears streaming down my face."

"Because of the isolation you experienced as trauma in your life in the past, you are more likely to interpret current situations like this stronger than someone who hadn't experienced those traumas. There will come a day where you can look at a post of people getting together without you and rejoice for them for their time together without feeling pain and focusing on how you weren't included."

"Yeah, I look forward to that day. I hate feeling triggered like this so often. I guess it feels like others have the love and connection I want and I'm on the outside looking in. I remember when I was on these forced visits with Harold, my real family back home, who I desperately wanted to be with, went on with life and activities together without me. I don't blame them. It's not like life can stop just because I was taken away, but knowing that they were together without me hurt so much, like my absence was insignificant. I would call my mom and ask what was happening. She would fill me in on all that was going on while I was away. She didn't want to hurt me; she just thought telling me about things and people I loved would take my mind off of the pain I was experiencing while away. Once, I remember my only uncle came to visit the family from thousands of miles away where he lived. The whole family would get together when he was there, getting to do fun outings and bonding when I was on a visitation with Harold. It felt isolating, like being imprisoned, but looking in from the outside. I would cry over all I was missing out on and how it felt like everyone went on without me during those weeks I was away. Of course, my mom's heart was always with me while I was gone but life went on and connection and bonding were occurring without me. Not only was it occurring without me but what I was experiencing was the exact opposite on my end. I felt completely out of control, isolated from love and comfort, and helpless to create change."

"And it is those very feelings that are being triggered by events today. If you are willing, let's go to the Lord in prayer and ask Him if it's true that you are isolated from love and helpless."

"I feel tremendous guilt about charging the necessary prices it takes to even break even in our business. I feel guilty when I'm not meeting others' desires. I want to bless people and want our clients to be happy but I'm also not able to sustain our business with constant discounts. For years, I have been sacrificing myself to avoid feeling bad and thinking I'm a burden. It has depleted my energy and financial resources and is now causing harm to my health, family, and finances. I also struggle with communicating my needs to others."

"Boundaries are so important," my counselor replied. "Why do you think you feel guilt over your legitimate needs?"

After talking about various instances in my life where I felt that my needs were a burden, we ultimately discussed the wound that originated these feelings.

"I always sensed I was a burden to Harold's family, not really one of their tribe yet having to be cared for as if I was. I felt this way with my own family as well at times. When my Mom was a single mom, she would leave me with some of her relatives during the summer while she worked. Though much more included in my family than his, I still felt an underlying resentment over my needs. Sometimes I was also not included in their activities, which felt isolating. Overall, I was left with the feeling that my needs and emotions were burdens to others and that they didn't really find joy in caring for me."

"Are there other times you don't feel like you are important to people you care about?"

"For some reason, it seems as though people only care about themselves or the work they are doing. I watch as others get so fired up over what they are doing and I truly rejoice with them. Yet when I start to share what's going on in my life and my work, it's like the twinkle in their eye starts to fade and they look disinterested. I ultimately feel insignificant, like my work is less important or smaller in value than what they do."

"Why do you think it matters to you for them to be interested in what is going on with you?"

"I suppose it is interpreted as valuable and therefore I am valuable."

"I see you want affirmation so badly, Sadie. Like you are grabbing for it with everything you've got. Yet, when it comes, it's like it hits a wall and falls to the ground. You don't take it in and receive it."

"I guess it's hard to receive from others most of the time. I question their motives. It's rare that I believe someone is giving me affirmation out of a pure place without having an ulterior motive. My relationship with Harold was confusing and likely served as a basis for me questioning others' motives. He would sometimes provide a gift or activity that would be fun for a child. But even those efforts ended up being part of his battle with my mom. He would come up with an activity he knew she wouldn't like, such as taking a flight with his brother, who was a pilot, and then, when she had a predictable reaction, he would assert his authority over me to do what he wanted in his time with me. When I would tell her of his plans, she would demand that I not do it. Then, when I told him my mom said I couldn't, he would demand that I would. This created such incredible chaos and anxiety in me because I never knew what was going to happen. Ultimately, I learned not to trust people's motives when providing me with something 'good.' I suppose that filters over into my ability to receive compliments or affirmations. I have a tendency to think, 'What do they really want?'"

"So really you are playing the role of God, determining the motives of the heart? What if instead you trusted the Lord to provide for your needs for affirmation and significance, thanking Him each time you received a compliment knowing that He allowed it regardless of the vessel's motives? What if you responded each time by taking it before the Lord and giving Him thanks and really taking it to heart?"

"I guess I hadn't really thought of it that way." From this point on, each time I received a compliment I slowed down, took it before the Lord in prayer and thanked Him for allowing it as a gift from Him. Determining the motive of the vessel was no longer my focus and I slowly began filling back up.

Counselors call situations that cause us pain "trigger" events. Something triggers areas in our brain where pain has happened before. So the pain we feel in a situation today is amplified by that same type of pain that we experienced in our past. Seemingly simple things can "trigger" my pain pathways: People shirking responsibility, delivery of low quality work, criticism, when others deviate from plans without discussing it with me, when people ignore rules, deception and injustice, etc. In all of these areas, a capacity for empathy and forgiveness can really help.

One area that seems to trigger me the most, however, is when I make mistakes. Every time I make a mistake or turn out to be incorrect or inaccurate in some way, I beat myself up with such ferocity that it's hard for me to emotionally recover from the weight of my own inner critic. I require constant comfort from others to feel okay about myself; the problem is, people can't carry the emotional burdens of others all of the time, or perhaps at all, and I was left feeling uncomfortable in my emotional turmoil a large part of the time. On top of that, I was wearing out my loved ones who were trying to carry me and my big emotions on top of the weight of their own burdens.

I was thankful for my counselor. Over time, she was able to shift my thinking and show me how to process pain myself with the Lord. She was there to help carry the burden of a triggering event each time it happened. Sometimes, the trigger would seem trivial, yet the feelings touched by the trigger were powerful.

She asked me, "How does this make you feel?"

"I feel defective, that something is intrinsically wrong with me, that I am 'not good enough.'"

"Are you willing to ask the Lord when you felt this way before?"

"Yes, I am willing."

"Father, you see Sadie right now. You see her pain and that she feels defective, wrong, and not good enough. In your grace and goodness, would you show her when she has felt this way before?"

We sat there together, silently waiting. Then she said, "Don't try to think about it, just tell me the first thing you hear, see, and think. Has anything come to you?"

"I see myself, about four years old, standing on my carport watching my father drive away."

"What else can you tell me about your biological father?"

"My mom married my biological father after a short dating period. In reality, they didn't know each other very well. Though he had revealed that he was sexually abused by his father as a child, she didn't realize the ramifications of that abuse and that he struggled with sexual dysfunction himself. Their marriage started off well as they were getting to know each other. She discovered she was pregnant with

166

me shortly after their honeymoon. Over time, however, there were signs that trouble was ahead.

"While away on a business trip, my father was unfaithful and returned home to reveal this to my mom. He tried saying he was just helping this other woman out, like he had just done her a favor. When my mom fell apart with a broken heart, he was unsupportive telling her that if she was going to be upset forever they might as well divorce.

"He began a variety of behaviors that made my mom feel unsafe. He started following cult teachings, invited vagrants into their home, continued his sexual transgressions, and remained largely unstable. Wanting to ensure our safety, Mom never allowed me to be alone with him and eventually chose to divorce."

"That's really scary and intense. Knowing this provides a lot of background for why your mom tried so hard to protect you from him. Can you tell me what you remember about when he left?"

"It's my earliest memory actually. I remember being in the carport. He had a recorder and was recording my voice. I remember there was the blinking red light on the recorder and I kept asking him what the light was. Somehow I sensed that this was the last time I was going to see my father. He was recording me to have the sound of my voice."

"So it was painful for him to leave you?"

"If actions express his feelings I'd have to say no. He agreed to give up his paternal rights when my grandfather adopted me just so he could get out of child support. Those payments were more valuable to him than I was. When he left, he took every possession they owned except for me and the TV. My mom fought him for a TV so I would have something to do, but he took everything else. He wanted every material possession they had, but he didn't want me. It's been hard not to interpret my value as less significant than material possessions. He had already taken his car and he came back to take my mom's car too, leaving us stranded. He took her car and he was in such a hurry to leave us that he backed out of the driveway and kept driving backwards all the way down the street. I wasn't worth fighting for and he drove away without me."

"You've come so far, Sadie. Tell me what you see."

"I see myself, about four years old, standing on my carport watching my Father drive away."

"Do you see anything else in this memory?"

"Yes, I do now. I see Jesus standing right beside me."

"What is he doing?"

"We are holding hands. He is watching me. And He doesn't seem surprised or worried."

"What are you doing?"

"I'm watching my father drive away."

"Sadie, turn and look at Jesus. Ask Him if you are really unwanted."

"I don't want to."

"Why don't you want to?"

"I want to watch my dad."

"Sadie, this can be your moment of healing. Turn your head, look at the Lord, and ask Him whether you are valuable. This is the breakthrough we have been working toward all these years."

At that moment, I finally turned and looked at my Savior. I took my attention away from my father driving backward down the street and I put it on Jesus. I asked him if it was true that I'm unwanted and need to be perfect, without mistakes, to be loved. And Jesus told me that my name means "Princess." He told me that I have an identity. That it is not "abandoned daughter" but "Daughter of the Most High King." He told me that I am precious to Him and anything done to hurt me is hurting the apple of His eye. He told me that He wants me and desires me and loves me more deeply than I can possibly imagine. The pure love of my Savior finally brought me healing when I turned my attention away from other people and toward Him. I had to drive backward through my life, through every hurt and pain and wrong, to get back to the original wounds that I had suffered as a little girl that left me feeling that I was not loved or wanted. With Jesus as the source of my fulfillment, like He should have been all along, I no longer had to look to people or friends or achievements and grasp for something that never really filled my need[3]. Only the Savior could truly and completely meet those needs and heal those wounds, and, when I finally turned to Him, that's exactly what He did. Now each time a triggering event occurs, I remind myself of this vision and turn my face toward Jesus.

More to Think About from Sadie

Sadie's story is somewhat different from the previous testimonies in this book. Her story goes more or less backwards in time as she works with a Christian counselor to reach the root of her insecurities and anxieties so that Christ can heal them. As she slowly deals with some of the traumas described, as well as others not mentioned in this story, she walks more and more in the freedom and joy of Christ. Ultimately, she comes to see that He was with her all along, that He was never surprised or overwhelmed by the things that happened to her, and that healing was always right there waiting for her. When she turned to Christ for fulfillment of her needs, Sadie finally began to heal and experience freedom. For some people there may be a stigma associated with counselling, but this should not be the case. Seeking counselling is like seeking any other kind of medical care and no one should ever be ashamed or embarrassed for seeking the care they need. Seeking godly counsel doesn't indicate a lack of faith, but shows maturity and humility in following what scripture tells us[4]. There are organizations like the American Association of Christian Counselors[5] and the Christian Counseling and Education Foundation[6] with many helpful resources. Proverbs 13:10 says, "Where there is strife, there is pride, but wisdom is found in those who take advice." If you or someone you know struggles with anxiety, depression, or other mental health issues, please seek help from a properly trained and licensed professional counselor.

Sadie also struggled with temptations in her life, temptations that touched on areas of perceived lack amplified by the traumas she had endured. But she had discovered that meditating on the Word of God helped her to respond appropriately and flee from these temptations. One that she mentioned was Proverbs 7, the warning against the adulterous woman. In other situations, other verses helped overcome temptation and rely on Jesus to meet her needs. The key is that she had spent time with God's Word, not just reading over it like a homework assignment, but memorizing and meditating on verses the Holy Spirit led her to. Temptation in life is unavoidable, but God has given us His Word to guide us away from the things that would destroy us and toward the things that bring life and to help us in every situation in life.

Prayer verse

1 Corinthians 10:13 (NIV) No temptation has overtaken you except what is common to mankind. And God is faithful; he will not let you be tempted beyond what you can bear. But when you are tempted, he will also provide a way out so that you can endure it.

Lord Jesus, You have been by my side all along, even when I didn't have eyes to see it. I know that You are the source of everything good in my life. I know that You are the only one who truly meets all my needs. My identity and worth can be found only in You. In the heat of every temptation, give me the wisdom, courage, and perseverance to walk away from sin and destruction and toward your marvelous light…

Jesus on the Road – Mark's Story

I was driving my truck down to Baton Rouge, Louisiana, to deliver a load of boats and trailers. It was the middle of the night; I couldn't pick up any radio stations as I drove along I-59 south of Meridian, Mississippi, and the CB radio and radar detector had been stolen from the truck. There were no distractions at all. That's when I saw it plain as day: Jesus Christ was walking down a cobblestone pathway. He was wearing a white robe with a gold rope tied around his waist[1]. It looked like a beautiful park in springtime with daffodils, tulips, and dogwoods. Little children were walking ahead of Him on the path with woven baskets throwing flower petals on the path. The Son of Almighty God was coming toward me, hair just below His shoulders, a light beard, gorgeous face, eyes that sparkled like blue diamonds, and a smile that would melt your heart. He spoke to me, like His voice was coming from the sleeper of my truck, and said, "Come follow Me."

I was born in Alabama in 1951. In all, there were six children: three older brothers and two younger sisters. My dad was a disabled veteran who fought in World War II. Now, they would say he had PTSD, but then I just knew he was a violent alcoholic whose drinking got worse and worse as the years went by. My three older brothers eventually moved off, leaving just me and my sisters at home. My dad would beat my mom and we would do what we could to try to keep him off of her.

I was eighteen years old when I graduated high school and got a job as a mechanic. I came home from a date one night that summer and Mother came into the bathroom where I was. I knew it must have been bad. My dad had dragged her out of the bed and threatened to kill her. The next morning, I asked my dad what he was going to do that day. He replied, and I said, "Well, how about you not get drunk today." He started cussing me, asking me "What business is it of yours if I get drunk?" "It's my business if you beat my mama and scare my sisters," I said. He started to reach in his pocket for his knife, which gave me a chance to take a swing at him. I hit him with all the built-up rage of eighteen years of abuse and knocked him across the room. He got up and started threatening to kill me, but I got nose to nose with him and said, "Look in my eyes, I've got you in me and I'm just as mean as you are. Don't you ever lay a hand on my mama again."

It was tough to confront him like that. It took courage. I believed he really could and would kill me. I didn't have to worry about his reaction for long. By September of that year, his alcoholism had killed him. Many years later, after I got to know Jesus, I realized that we are supposed to love our mother and father[2]. The Lord gave me a dream in which I saw my father in heaven, with his head hung in shame over everything he had done. I wrapped my arms around him and told him I loved him. Just like that my anger and bitterness toward him were gone. I had always wanted to pour whiskey on his grave and tell him how mad I was, but God healed me from that pain.

When I was in junior high, I went on a double date with a buddy of mine and two girls who went to a local church. My friend decided we ought to try going to church too and we went that Sunday. It was so unexpected for me to show up at church that the girl I had gone out with saw me and screamed and ran the other way. All the kids from the local high schools went there and they had a big youth group. With everything I had going on at home, I needed that type of group, so I kept going to church. I eventually joined the church and got baptized there on Mother's Day; my mother came to watch me get baptized and realized a lot of people she knew went to church there. Most of my family ended up attending off and on with me. The Lord had His hand on me the whole time.

After my dad died, I took classes at the local community college and worked at an auto parts store. I had a really cool Honda motorcycle that I rode everywhere. I was riding down University Drive in Huntsville, Alabama, doing about 55 mph in the left lane with a car beside me in the right lane. Another car hadn't seen me and pulled onto the road right in front of me. There was nothing I could do; I made eye contact with the guy riding in the back seat as I hit the car doing 55. Suddenly it was like I was in the front row of a movie theater watching my life flash in front of me. I was dead and gone; I was in a dark tunnel flying toward a bright light. Then I heard a loud voice say, "Go back; it's not your time."

I flipped in the air as I flew over the car, landed on my neck and shoulders, and flopped all around on the pavement. I remember my helmet slamming the pavement. It should have broken my neck. It was 9:30 on a Saturday night on a busy road, so I started crawling over to the gravel on the side of the road. I started checking my extremities; at first I couldn't feel my right leg below the knee. The guy who hit me took off into the housing projects nearby. People kept passing by until eventually a soldier from the local Army Post stopped to help. In the end I walked away with no loss of blood and no broken bones. I even helped the guy load my motorcycle onto the wrecker that came. My life had been miraculously spared.

That big motorcycle crash was in 1971. I had another motorcycle wreck in 1985; that time, I had torn ligaments and was left with pain in both knees that stayed with me for years. Mostly, though, life just kept cruising along. I got married twice, divorced twice, and had a son. Around 1990, almost twenty years later, I started seeking the Lord. I wanted to know why I had survived that crash. Why did He send me back? I had been going to the same church but had not been very involved. God was drawing me closer to Him and He was getting me ready for radical changes in my life.

I had a friend named Kent who I had worked with. We stayed close and would travel to bike week in Daytona together every year. Kent met a spirit-filled lady who went to a local charismatic church[3] and he would stay with me on the weekends and go to church with her. At one of their church picnics, Kent met a pretty little lady named Gail, who was divorced, and he got her phone number for me. He gave me her number and said, "Here it is, but you better not go over there drinking a beer or anything because she'll whip you." I decided I would pass; I didn't want God mad at me for messing up with a good Christian woman.

Kent got engaged to the woman he had been seeing, and, one day, his fiancée called me and said she had a problem. She told me she had prayed about it and the Lord told her to call me. That seemed pretty hard to believe, but it turned out that the Lord had prepared me without me knowing it. Kent and I had learned how to repair water heaters and I was pretty good at it. Now his fiancée told me that she knew a lady at church who was divorced with two kids. She worked at a pizza place and didn't have any homeowners insurance or money to repair her broken water heater. If I would fix it, Kent's fiancée would pay for the parts. That was a problem I could help with.

I went over to the house and it turned out it was Gail, the woman I had decided not to call. She told me that she didn't date anyway and that the Lord would bring the right man at the right time if she was supposed to marry again. I fixed the water heater, worked on her car, and fixed all sorts of things around her house. Now, this is not a love story about Gail and me. We never did have that kind of relationship; in fact, a few years later, I was honored to give her away at her wedding.

They were all praying for me and I continued questioning the Lord about why I had survived that wreck so many years ago. I had been to a few different kinds of churches over the years, but never a spirit-filled charismatic church. Kent was married at that charismatic church and I was his best man. Eventually I attended some services there, and, when I went in, they were praising God in a way

I had never seen before. They were really into it and I could feel the joy of the Holy Spirit there.

The night before Good Friday 1991, I was delivering bass boats for Challenger Boats, and preparing to leave Fayetteville, Tennessee, for Baton Rouge, Louisiana. The weather was bad and I heard there was a tornado around Florence, Alabama, so I decided to go down through Huntsville instead. About the time I arrived at the state line, I heard there was a tornado over Madison, Alabama that was heading my direction. I pulled my truck up beside a big brick church building to wait it out; if I was going to go, I wanted it to happen at the Lord's house. The owner of the boat company drove by and saw me and asked what I was doing. I told him that I was going to wait out the storm and he just laughed and said I could wait until the weather cleared before I got back on the road. Someone had stolen my CB radio the week before and that day another thief had stolen my radar detector, so the only thing I had in the truck was the AM/FM radio. Little did I know God had arranged for me to be on the road late at night, with nobody else on the road and with no distractions.

I was south of Meridian, Mississippi when I had the vision of Jesus. There was no radio station in range, everything else in my truck that made noise had been stolen, and I was the only one on the road. In fact, I drove over 200 miles between Meridian and Baton Rouge without seeing another vehicle. The weigh stations, which were always open, had closed that night. The Lord had me all to Himself. I saw Him on that path in the park, children in front of Him dropping flower petals, and a whole line of people behind Him. "Come follow Me," He said.

I was just blown away. Suddenly all the stories from the Bible became reality to me. They weren't just stories anymore; they were real. As I saw the Lord, I stepped into that reality. I heard the voice that sounded like it was coming from the sleeper of my truck. "Mark, this is my Son Jesus. I'm ready to send Him back, but the world isn't ready for Him. You're not ready for Him." My spirit man left the truck and went up to the sky; I could still see my physical body driving the truck as I left it.

For hours, as my physical body drove all those miles with nobody else around, He shared so many sights with me. He took me up to the edge of space, where I could see the earth, and I saw a black cloud over the U.S. He showed me that the cloud represented illegal drugs and that 85% of crime could be attributed to substance abuse. He showed me old people afraid to leave their homes and young people who saw no future for themselves but darkness. He said, "They have cried out and I have heard their cries; I need you to go to work for Me, Mark." "I don't know You that well," I said. "You will," He said. "I haven't even read the Bible all the way through," I said. "You have time," He said. He showed me a plan to treat substance abuse as a sickness rather than a crime, with clinics to help people rather than throwing them in jail where they would get no help. He showed me the plan, which continues to unfold in His perfect timing.

I made it to Baton Rouge and unloaded the boats and trailers early that morning. I completed the paperwork and left, thinking I would stop at the first rest area and get some sleep after my long night. Instead, the Holy Spirit started right back where we had left off, continuing to share His plans with me. It was a two-way conversation, like He was sitting there in the truck with me. I was around Hattiesburg, Mississippi, when I decided to put down a fleece like Gideon[4] in the Old Testament to make sure I was really hearing from the Lord. "This is some heavy stuff, Lord; show me this is really you," I told Him. In my flesh[5], my worldly thinking, I said it will take money to do some of these things and I know there's a dog track just across the state line so show me a longshot to put a bunch of money on. "You can do better than that," the Lord told me.

I was getting close to Tuscaloosa, Alabama, when I realized what I should ask for. My friend Gail had a serious problem with her right ear. For three years it stayed infected; she always had cotton in it and couldn't hear out of it. She had gone to a specialist in Birmingham, the only one in the Southeast at that time, and he had said only surgery could fix that ear. She didn't have insurance or enough money to pay for it and he insisted he wouldn't do the surgery for free. So she continued on with no relief. She had told God that she would depend on Him for healing.

I said, "Lord, you know that Gail has this problem with her ear. Heal her ear as a sign between me and you." I felt God smile and say, "That's more my style." The Holy Spirit was on me so heavily that I just wanted to cry. "Lord, why now?" I asked. "This is Easter. Isn't this a time for miracles?" He replied. I pulled into a rest area outside Tuscaloosa and just cried and cried until I was soaked with tears.

The Lord told me to get up and go on home, so I started back out on the road. I was coming down the long hill just before I-459 splits off to go around Birmingham; there was no air conditioning in the truck so I had the window down and the wind was blowing in my left ear. Suddenly I felt intense burning in my right ear, like somebody was holding a torch up to it. I cried out to God and He said, "What did you ask of Me?" "Oh Lord, you are healing her ear, let it burn!"

I made it back to Fayetteville to drop my truck off and called my mom. She said she was going to Good Friday services at the church and I told her I would meet her there. I had tried to get in touch with Gail, but she didn't answer. I went to meet my mom at the service. I could still feel the mighty presence of the Lord beside me as I walked in. I felt like I was floating, and, for the first time since my 1985 motorcycle crash, my knees didn't hurt at all. As I went in, the choir was on the left, already singing, with a cross and candelabra in front. Everyone in the church turned and looked at me when I came in the door. I thought, "Are they looking at me or do they see Him with me?" There were three people who witnessed it. The lady who was working the lights told me that, when I walked in, there was an awesome presence with me that led me all the way in and to a particular seat. She said everyone in the room looked, but only a portion of them understood what they were feeling. The choir director said almost exactly the same thing, that there was an awesome presence with me, that everyone looked and felt something, but that not all of them knew what it was. Another lady told my mother that when I walked in, there was a huge angel walking right beside me. We were all in God's presence in that service[6].

The Good Friday service focused on the last seven words of Christ on the cross[7]. The candelabra in front had seven candles; the pastor would read a verse, a candle would be lit, and the lights would be dimmed. The Lord spoke to me again and said, "Mark, I want you down at the foot of that cross begging forgiveness for your sins." I argued with Him, "Lord, I've been here twenty years and I've never seen anybody do anything like that." The lights would dim for a new candle, the Lord would repeat His command, and I would argue. The choir started singing "Were You There When They Crucified My Lord" and I felt like He jerked me out of my seat and threw me all the way up to the foot of the cross. Mother said it looked like I ran up there. I cried out, "Lord, forgive me: I have sinned!" As I cried out, I was afraid the people in the church would think I had committed some terrible crime. But I started to feel hands on my back and shoulders; in the end, half of the church was there kneeling with me.

After the service, the pastor, Brother Travis, said, "Mark, I'd like to hear this story, can you meet me in my office tomorrow morning?" After the service, I went to my mother's house and explained everything that had happened. Her phone rang off the hook with people from the church calling to ask her about it. Saturday morning, I met with Brother Travis and told him all about it. He said, "God's will be done," and prayed in agreement with me. Finally, I went to Gail's house and her daughter let me in. I asked how her ear was. She looked at me like I was glowing and said, "Come sit at the table. Something happened, didn't it?" I asked again about her ear. It had been about ten minutes before 7:00 when I went to the cross at the Good Friday service the night before. She then told me, "Last night, I was rushing to get to a 7 pm Good Friday service in Decatur, when suddenly my ear popped, fluid drained out of it, and I could hear for the first time in three years. Now tell me what happened!" I told her my whole story, all the way through going up to the cross to beg forgiveness. That was the time at which her ear was healed. Gail told me, "I've been to every prayer meeting and evangelist. I knew God could heal me, but I didn't know why He hadn't yet. Now I know it was waiting for you. I knew you were a good man when I met you, but you didn't truly know Him yet."

After that Good Friday, God really got hold of me. I was driving my truck to Tulsa and, somewhere between Memphis and Little Rock, I saw the most tremendous lightning storm I have ever witnessed. I was in awe of the mighty power of God. I spoke to God and said, "Lord I know You have done something in me, You called me, Lord, I'm trying. Lord, do I have the power to pray and see people be healed?" His reply came quickly, "The power is within you by the Holy Spirit[8]. Your job is to pray; when they are healed is up to Me."

I had a regular run to Tampa, Florida, where there was a Vietnam veteran named Jimmy who unloaded the truck. I got there one day and Jimmy's eye was in really bad shape. He thought it was just pink eye, but it looked a lot worse than that. He knew a little bit about me, so I told him when we got done unloading that I would pray for his eye. "My name's not Jesus," I told him, "But I know Him and He is the healer, not me." I prayed for him and went on my way. Two weeks later, I was there again, and, when I pulled in, Jimmy came running across the parking lot as fast as he could go, yelling for me. "Mark! Mark! It's better! It's better!" He took his sunglasses off and said he could see now. "Wait a minute, you couldn't see?" "No, but I can now," he told me. "Thank God, not me," I told him, "I'm just a tool in His toolbox."

The next time I went to Tampa, Jimmy asked if I was going to park in my usual spot across the road in front of a row of restaurants. I asked why and he told me he had a lady friend who was in really bad shape. Jimmy sent me off with another guy named Sidney to go see Miss Daisy, who was bedridden. I didn't know what I was getting into, so I prayed for protection the whole way up there. It turned out Daisy was Sidney's ex-wife, but he was still trying to help her. She was lying in bed with tuberculosis; according to the doctor, her right lung was completely dead and she was too weak to operate on. She had a suction tube pulling fluid out of that lung into a drain tube and she was on six different types of medication for infection and pain. Daisy looked at me and said, "I believe the Lord can heal me." "That is faith," I told her. I gave her my testimony, anointed her with oil as they did in the Bible, and prayed for healing. I turned and said, "What about you, Sidney?" He said, "I'm not as close to the Lord as I need to be; I need help getting a job." We prayed for his drinking problem and for a job.

Three weeks later, I was back and I asked how she was doing. "Oh, she's doing fine," Sidney said, "She can go up and down the stairs and walk to the store by herself now." The next time I was in Tampa I went to see her and she met me at the door. She told me what happened after I had prayed over her: she started having trouble with the drain tube so they put her in the hospital. She showed me the scar where they had cut her open. It turned out the tube had to come out for her to get completely healed. They pulled the lung partway out, removed the tube, scraped the lung, put it back in, and sewed her up. The lung that had been dead was completely healed and she no longer needed any medication for pain or for tuberculosis. The Lord had miraculously healed her.

Back at home, I had a neighbor named Barry who had cancer. I had witnessed to Barry before but he always pushed me away. I don't push the Lord on anyone; I offer and they can choose whether to accept. Barry had been sick before, and had lost a kidney; four years later, the cancer was back. I had a buddy I worked on race cars with who also knew Barry. I had told both him and his wife my testimony and she was moved to tears by it. It was the 4th of July, 2006, and we were at the drag strip. My buddy's wife said, "Have you seen Barry? He's in bad shape: the cancer is back. He's been asking about you." The little seeds of faith I had planted before were ready to sprout[9].

The next day, I was on the front porch when Barry came driving up. "I heard a bad report about your health," I said. He had an inoperable tumor between his heart and lung. His chest was swollen with fluid. Five times they had drained 1.5L of fluid from around his heart. He had been to a specialist at Vanderbilt, who told him to get his affairs in order because they couldn't operate and they couldn't do chemo since his kidneys were already so diminished. They prescribed him some experimental pills and sent him home. He had cried out to God and heard a voice tell him to come and see me. I said, "Barry, let me tell you about Dr. Jesus." "I know you've been trying to tell me about Him," Barry said. I told him my testimony. He was crying but he tried to pretend he was just wiping sweat away. We went inside to pray. He said he had actually been saved and baptized as a child, but we went through the sinner's prayer to make sure he was in right standing first. Then we prayed for healing.

The next day I was driving home and felt the Lord say to stop at the Dollar General. I went in and Barry was there waiting for UPS to deliver his $6,000 experimental pills. I laughed and said I hadn't seen him in months and now I've seen him twice in two days. There had been so much fluid swelling his chest that he had not even been able to bend down and wash his feet in the shower. That morning, he got up and all that fluid was gone. Barry was completely healed.

Jimmy and Daisy and Barry are just a few examples of people God has miraculously healed over the years. While I was driving a truck, the Lord put me on the road for two million miles and He taught me. I've seen blind eyes healed, deaf ears opened, and stammering tongues loosed. With every one, I make sure they know first that Jesus is the one healing them, not me. It is only through His power that anybody can be healed. If God can use this old country boy like that, He can use you too.

More to Think About from Mark

Mark had the kind of supernatural encounter with the Almighty that few of us will ever experience. God speaks through the Holy Spirit in many ways, some subtle and some not, and, in reality, we have all heard from the Holy Spirit in one way or another. Mark was not living an incredibly spiritual life before his experience with Christ. Mark didn't have any fancy credentials or seminary degrees, nor did he go get those things after his experience. The one ability Mark had was availability, really the only thing God needs from us. He does His best work in our weaknesses when we simply rely on Him rather than our strengths or achievements.

1 Corinthians 12:8-10 says, "To one there is given through the Spirit a message of wisdom, to another a message of knowledge by means of the same Spirit, to another faith by the same Spirit, to another gifts of healing by that one Spirit, to another miraculous powers, to another prophecy, to another distinguishing between spirits, to another speaking in different kinds of tongues, and to still another the interpretation of tongues." James 5:14-15 says, "Is anyone among you sick? Let them call the elders of the church to pray over them and anoint them with oil in the name of the Lord. And the prayer offered in faith will make the sick person well; the Lord will raise them up. If they have sinned, they will be forgiven." There are dozens of scriptures about healing and other gifts of the Holy Spirit. Every believer, through the Holy Spirit, has the same power living in us that raised Christ from the dead. We simply have to pray and believe in alignment with the sovereign will of God.

God's ability to heal supernaturally doesn't mean that we eschew doctors and medicine; after all, God provided the wisdom for those things as well and Luke the physician[10] traveled along with the Apostle Paul. God heals in four ways: He created our bodies to heal themselves and His creation is miraculous in its own right. He is the source of all knowledge, so all of the doctors and researchers of modern medicine are also His agents of healing whether they realize it or not. Most of the time, God's healing comes through these everyday forms. But the Great Physician[11] is still greater than any earthly physician and there are times like the ones Mark described that He steps in supernaturally to heal someone in a spectacular way. Finally, all believers receive ultimate healing in heaven. God in His infallible wisdom chooses to leave some people unhealed. The Apostle Paul described a thorn in his side that is believed to be a physical ailment; God did not heal it on earth but rather told Paul that His grace was sufficient. It is up to God whether He heals someone through natural or human means, supernaturally through a miracle, or ultimately in heaven after they leave the earth; we simply pray in faith and believe in His perfect healing in His perfect timing.

Prayer verse

Isaiah 53:5 (NIV) But he was pierced for our transgressions, he was crushed for our iniquities; the punishment that brought us peace was on him, and by his wounds we are healed.

Lord Jesus, I believe in You and You are the Lord of my life. I know that the Holy Spirit dwells in me and that the same power that raised You from the dead now lives in me. Your Holy Word says that by your stripes we are healed. I pray right now in your name, by the power of the Holy Spirit, for healing …

Afterword

In this book you have read eight true stories of God's amazing grace. You have read about how He can save us from the deepest despair and the most severe traumas and work miracles in our lives. The first thing is the most important: Pray your own version of a sinner's prayer and accept Jesus Christ as Lord of your life. Then commit yourself to Bible study and prayer, and follow in obedience where the Holy Spirit leads. Seek the help that you need, whether it is help with addictions, grief, forgiveness, or mental health issues. As you find the healing that comes only from Jesus, begin to share your joy with others. Make yourself available for God to use you in mighty ways as you surrender to Him. A life with Christ may not always be safe and predictable, but it is never boring, for it is the most rewarding way to live. In the end, the greatest rewards are in store for us when this life is done.

The Apostle Paul, 2 Corinthians 11:24-27 (NIV): Five times I received from the Jews the forty lashes minus one. Three times I was beaten with rods, once I was pelted with stones, three times I was shipwrecked, I spent a night and a day in the open sea, I have been constantly on the move. I have been in danger from rivers, in danger from bandits, in danger from my fellow Jews, in danger from Gentiles; in danger in the city, in danger in the country, in danger at sea; and in danger from false believers. I have labored and toiled and have often gone without sleep; I have known hunger and thirst and have often gone without food; I have been cold and naked.

The Apostle Paul, 2 Timothy 4:7-8 (NIV): I have fought the good fight, I have finished the race, I have kept the faith. Now there is in store for me the crown of righteousness, which the Lord, the righteous Judge, will award to me on that day—and not only to me, but also to all who have longed for his appearing.

References and Resources

This section lists the numbered scripture references, books, and other resources from throughout the book. Scriptures that were included in their entirety in the text of the book are not listed here. A reference is only numbered and listed on its first mention.

Ashleigh Grace

1. Generational curses are particular sins and hardships that persist in a family from generation to generation. Many verses touch on this concept. Jeremiah 31:29-30 (NIV) "In those days people will no longer say, 'The parents have eaten sour grapes, and the children's teeth are set on edge.' Instead, everyone will die for their own sin; whoever eats sour grapes—their own teeth will be set on edge." Proverbs 26:2 (NIV) Like a fluttering sparrow or a darting swallow, an undeserved curse does not come to rest.

2. Romans 5:3-5 (NIV) Not only so, but we also glory in our sufferings, because we know that suffering produces perseverance; perseverance, character; and character, hope. And hope does not put us to shame, because God's love has been poured out into our hearts through the Holy Spirit, who has been given to us.

195

3. John 6:44 (NIV) No one can come to me unless the Father who sent me draws them, and I will raise them up at the last day.

4. 1 John 3:1 (NIV) See what great love the Father has lavished on us, that we should be called children of God! And that is what we are! The reason the world does not know us is that it did not know him.

5. Psalm 40:2 (NIV) He lifted me out of the slimy pit, out of the mud and mire; he set my feet on a rock and gave me a firm place to stand. 2 Corinthians 1:10 (NIV) He has delivered us from such a deadly peril, and he will deliver us again. On him we have set our hope that he will continue to deliver us.

6. Lecrae official website: https://www.lecrae.com/

7. *The Ultimate Treasure Hunt: A Guide to Supernatural Evangelism Through Supernatural Encounters*, by Kevin Dedmon, from Destiny Image.

8. Matthew 19:9 (NIV) I tell you that anyone who divorces his wife, except for sexual immorality, and marries another woman commits adultery.

9. Proverbs 6:31 (NIV) Yet if he is caught, he must pay sevenfold, though it costs him all the wealth of his house.

10. The Romans Road to Salvation is a series of verses from Paul's epistle to the church at Rome that describe the need for and path to salvation. These verses include Romans 3:23, Romans 6:23, Romans 5:8, Romans 10:9-10, and Romans 10:13. Some evangelists include additional verses as well.

Whit

1. The Gideon's International official website: https://www.gideons.org/

2. Vacation Bible School is typically a week-long summer program for children to learn about Christianity. The concept originated in the late 19th century and remains popular today.

3. Conviction is the feeling of wrongdoing brought by the Holy Spirit. John 16:8 (NIV) When he comes, he will prove the world to be in the wrong about sin and righteousness and judgment.

4. Kairos Prison Ministry International official website: http://www.kairosprisonministry.org/

5. Apologetics comes from the Greek word *apologia* as used in 1 Peter 3:15 (NIV) But in your hearts revere Christ as Lord. Always be prepared to give an answer to

everyone who asks you to give the reason for the hope that you have. But do this with gentleness and respect.

6. The *Truth Project* video series from Focus on the Family: https://www.focusonthefamily.com/faith/the-truth-project/

7. *Foundations of Apologetics* video series from Ravi Zacharias International Ministries: https://www.rzim.org/

8. *Mere Christianity*, by C.S. Lewis, from HarperOne.

9. *The Case for Christ: A Journalist's Personal Investigation of the Evidence for Jesus*, by Lee Strobel, from Zondervan.

10. *The New Evidence That Demands A Verdict: Evidence I & II Fully Updated in One Volume To Answer The Questions Challenging Christians in the 21st Century*, by Josh McDowell, from Thomas Nelson Inc.

11. *Cold-Case Christianity: A Homicide Detective Investigates the Claims of the Gospels*, by J. Warner Wallace, from David C Cook.

12. *On Guard: Defending Your Faith with Reason and Precision*, by William Lane Craig, from David C Cook.

13. *God's Not Dead: Evidence for God in an Age of Uncertainty*, by Rice Brooks, from Thomas Nelson Inc.

14. *Mama Bear Apologetics™: Empowering Your Kids to Challenge Cultural Lies*, by Hillary Morgan Ferrer, from Harvest House Publishers.

15. Psalm 49:3 (NIV) My mouth will speak words of wisdom; the meditation of my heart will give you understanding.

16. *Healing Your Church Hurt: What To Do When You Still Love God But Have Been Wounded by His People*, by Stephen Mansfield, from Tyndale Momentum.

Tiffany

1. The New Living Translation is a paraphrase from Tyndale House Publishers. NLT Study Bible: http://nltstudybible.com/

2. Mark 16:20 (NIV) Then the disciples went out and preached everywhere, and the Lord worked with them and confirmed his word by the signs that accompanied it.

3. Philippians 3:13 (NIV) Brothers and sisters, I do not consider myself yet to have taken hold of it. But one thing I do: Forgetting what is behind and straining toward what is ahead.

4. Acts 9:1-6 (NIV) Meanwhile, Saul was still breathing out murderous threats against the Lord's disciples. He went to the high priest and asked him for letters to the

synagogues in Damascus, so that if he found any there who belonged to the Way, whether men or women, he might take them as prisoners to Jerusalem. As he neared Damascus on his journey, suddenly a light from heaven flashed around him. He fell to the ground and heard a voice say to him, "Saul, Saul, why do you persecute me?" "Who are you, Lord?" Saul asked. "I am Jesus, whom you are persecuting," he replied. "Now get up and go into the city, and you will be told what you must do."

5. 2 Samuel 11:14-15 (NIV) In the morning David wrote a letter to Joab and sent it with Uriah. In it he wrote, "Put Uriah out in front where the fighting is fiercest. Then withdraw from him so he will be struck down and die."

6. *Unstuck* audio series by Chip Ingram: https://livingontheedge.org/broadcast-series/unstuck/

7. *Overcomer: 8 Ways to Live a Life of Unstoppable Strength, Unmovable Faith, and Unbelievable Power,* by Dr. David Jeremiah, from Thomas Nelson Inc.

8. *It's Not Supposed to Be This Way: Finding Unexpected Strength When Disappointments Leave You Shattered,* by Lysa TerKeurst, from Thomas Nelson.

9. Care Network Crisis Pregnancy Centers: https://www.care-net.org/what-is-a-pregnancy-center

10. Heartbeat International:
https://www.heartbeatinternational.org/

Barry

1. Hebrews 12:10-11 (NIV) They disciplined us for a little while as they thought best; but God disciplines us for our good, in order that we may share in his holiness. No discipline seems pleasant at the time, but painful. Later on, however, it produces a harvest of righteousness and peace for those who have been trained by it.

2. Teen Challenge USA: https://teenchallengeusa.org/

3. Luke 3:16 (NIV) John answered them all, "I baptize you with water. But one who is more powerful than I will come, the straps of whose sandals I am not worthy to untie. He will baptize you with the Holy Spirit and fire. Acts 1:8 (NIV) But you will receive power when the Holy Spirit comes on you; and you will be my witnesses in Jerusalem, and in all Judea and Samaria, and to the ends of the earth.

4. The *Million Dollar Gospel* tract is a classic distributed by many organizations. This is just one example:
http://store.livingwaters.com/gospel-tracts/million-dollar-bill.html

5. Philippians 4:7 (NIV) And the peace of God, which transcends all understanding, will guard your hearts and your minds in Christ Jesus.

6. Celebrate Recovery, a Christ-centered 12-step Program: https://www.celebraterecovery.com/

7. *The Normal Christian Life*, by Watchman Nee, from Christian Literature Crusade.

8. Philippians 2:12 (NIV) Therefore, my dear friends, as you have always obeyed—not only in my presence, but now much more in my absence—continue to work out your salvation with fear and trembling.

9. John 19:30 (NIV) When he had received the drink, Jesus said, "It is finished." With that, he bowed his head and gave up his spirit.

10. *The Cross and the Switchblade*, by David Wilkerson, from Berkley.

11. John 14:26 (NIV) But the Advocate, the Holy Spirit, whom the Father will send in my name, will teach you all things and will remind you of everything I have said to you.

12. Philippians 1:6 (NIV) being confident of this, that he who began a good work in you will carry it on to completion until the day of Christ Jesus.

Lauren

1. Joyce Meyer Ministries: https://joycemeyer.org/

2. 2 Corinthians 12:7b-9 (NIV) Therefore, in order to keep me from becoming conceited, I was given a thorn in my flesh, a messenger of Satan, to torment me. Three times I pleaded with the Lord to take it away from me. But he said to me, "My grace is sufficient for you, for my power is made perfect in weakness." Therefore I will boast all the more gladly about my weaknesses, so that Christ's power may rest on me.

3. There are many versions of a sinner's prayer for salvation. This example is from Dr. Ray Pritchard: Lord Jesus, for too long I've kept you out of my life. I know that I am a sinner and that I cannot save myself. No longer will I close the door when I hear you knocking. By faith I gratefully receive your gift of salvation. I am ready to trust you as my Lord and Savior. Thank you, Lord Jesus, for coming to earth. I believe you are the Son of God who died on the cross for my sins and rose from the dead on the third day. Thank you for bearing my sins and giving me the gift of eternal life. I believe your words are true. Come into my heart, Lord Jesus, and be my Savior. Amen.

4. Proverbs 19:20 (NIV) Listen to advice and accept discipline, and at the end you will be counted among the wise.

5. Philippians 4:13 (NIV) I can do all this through him who gives me strength.

6. John 10:10 (NIV) The thief comes only to steal and kill and destroy; I have come that they may have life, and have it to the full.

7. *The Problem of Pain*, by C.S. Lewis, from HarperOne.

8. To Write Love on Her Arms: https://twloha.com/

9. National Suicide Prevention Lifeline: 1-800-273-8255, chat at https://suicidepreventionlifeline.org/

Ken

1. Jonah 1:17 (NIV) Now the Lord provided a huge fish to swallow Jonah, and Jonah was in the belly of the fish three days and three nights.

2. Daniel 6:19-22 (NIV) At the first light of dawn, the king got up and hurried to the lions' den. When he came near the den, he called to Daniel in an anguished voice, "Daniel, servant of the living God, has your God, whom you serve continually, been able to rescue you from the lions?" Daniel answered, "May the king live forever! My

God sent his angel, and he shut the mouths of the lions. They have not hurt me, because I was found innocent in his sight. Nor have I ever done any wrong before you, Your Majesty."

3. Luke 2:7b (NIV) She wrapped him in cloths and placed him in a manger, because there was no guest room available for them.

4. Romans 8:28 (NIV) And we know that in all things God works for the good of those who love him, who have been called according to his purpose.

5. Galatians 3:26 (NIV) So in Christ Jesus you are all children of God through faith.

6. Walk to Emmaus: http://emmaus.upperroom.org/

7. Jesus' parable of the workers in the field teaches that even those who pray for salvation at the last minute will receive it. Matthew 20:12-15 (NIV) 'These who were hired last worked only one hour,' they said, 'and you have made them equal to us who have borne the burden of the work and the heat of the day.' "But he answered one of them, 'I am not being unfair to you, friend. Didn't you agree to work for a denarius? Take your pay and go. I want to give the one who was hired last the same as I gave you. Don't I have the right to do what I want with my own money? Or are you envious because I am generous?'

8. The Lord's Prayer, Matthew 6:9-15 (NIV) "This, then, is how you should pray: "'Our Father in heaven, hallowed be your name, your kingdom come, your will be done, on earth as it is in heaven. Give us today our daily bread. And forgive us our debts, as we also have forgiven our debtors. And lead us not into temptation, but deliver us from the evil one.' For if you forgive other people when they sin against you, your heavenly Father will also forgive you. But if you do not forgive others their sins, your Father will not forgive your sins.

9. *The Forgiveness of God*, by Mart DeHaan: https://discoveryseries.org/courses/the-forgiveness-of-god/

10. *Total Forgiveness: When Everything in You Wants to Hold a Grudge, Point a Finger, and Remember the Pain-God Wants You to Lay it All Aside*, by R.T. Kendall, from Charisma House.

11. *Helping People Forgive*, by David W. Augsburger, from Westminster John Knox Press.

12. *Five Steps to Forgiveness: The Art and Science of Forgiving*, by Everett Worthington, from Crown.

Sadie

1. The type of counselling described in this story is Theophistic Prayer Ministry. No endorsement is made for or against this or any other counselling program.

2. Proverbs 7:24-27 (NIV) Now then, my sons, listen to me; pay attention to what I say. Do not let your heart turn to her ways or stray into her paths. Many are the victims she has brought down; her slain are a mighty throng. Her house is a highway to the grave, leading down to the chambers of death.

3. 1 Corinthians 8:6 (NIV) yet for us there is but one God, the Father, from whom all things came and for whom we live; and there is but one Lord, Jesus Christ, through whom all things came and through whom we live.

4. Proverbs 12:15 (NIV) The way of fools seems right to them, but the wise listen to advice.

5. American Association of Christian Counselors: https://www.aacc.net/

6. Christian Counseling and Education Foundation: https://www.ccef.org/

REFERENCES AND RESOURCES

Mark

1. Revelation 1:13 (NIV) and among the lampstands was someone like a son of man, dressed in a robe reaching down to his feet and with a golden sash around his chest.

2. Exodus 20:12 (NIV) Honor your father and your mother, so that you may live long in the land the Lord your God is giving you.

3. Charismatic churches are those that place an emphasis on the gifts of the Holy Spirit, such as speaking in tongues and prophecy.

4. Judges 6:36-40 (NIV) Gideon said to God, "If you will save Israel by my hand as you have promised— look, I will place a wool fleece on the threshing floor. If there is dew only on the fleece and all the ground is dry, then I will know that you will save Israel by my hand, as you said." And that is what happened. Gideon rose early the next day; he squeezed the fleece and wrung out the dew— a bowlful of water. Then Gideon said to God, "Do not be angry with me. Let me make just one more request. Allow me one more test with the fleece, but this time make the fleece dry and let the ground be covered with dew." That night God did so. Only the fleece was dry; all the ground was covered with dew.

5. Matthew 26:41 (NIV) "Watch and pray so that you will not fall into temptation. The spirit is willing, but the flesh is weak."

6. Isaiah 63:9a (NIV) In all their distress he too was distressed, and the angel of his presence saved them.

7. "The Last Seven Words of Christ" is a common liturgy practiced on Good Friday. One example may be found here: https://www.jesuschristsavior.net/Words.html

8. Romans 8:10-11 (NIV) But if Christ is in you, then even though your body is subject to death because of sin, the Spirit gives life because of righteousness. And if the Spirit of him who raised Jesus from the dead is living in you, he who raised Christ from the dead will also give life to your mortal bodies because of his Spirit who lives in you.

9. 1 Corinthians 3:7-9 (NIV) So neither the one who plants nor the one who waters is anything, but only God, who makes things grow. The one who plants and the one who waters have one purpose, and they will each be rewarded according to their own labor. For we are co-workers in God's service; you are God's field, God's building.

10. Colossians 4:14 (NIV) Our dear friend Luke, the doctor, and Demas send greetings.

11. Psalm 147:3 (NIV) He heals the brokenhearted and binds up their wounds.

About the Author

Son of a criminal sentenced to death, Dr. Chris Brown writes from his extensive experience of witnessing God's grace in the most unlikely circumstances. Chris has shared his message of hope both at home and abroad, with the free and the incarcerated, showing all that they are not too far gone, too lost, or too broken to be accepted and lovingly restored by God. Chris' unique experience and love for God have allowed him to share remarkable true stories of God's grace in action.

www.childofgracebooks.com

CPSIA information can be obtained
at www.ICGtesting.com
Printed in the USA
FSHW011815100920